How To
Heal with Color

About the Author

Ted Andrews was a full-time author and teacher in the metaphysical and spiritual fields. He conducted seminars, symposiums, workshops, and lectures throughout the U.S., Europe, and parts of Asia on many facets of ancient mysticism. Ted worked with past-life analysis, auric interpretation, numerology, the tarot, and the Qabala as methods of developing and enhancing inner potential. He was a clairvoyant certified in spiritual mediumship, basic hypnosis, and acupressure. Ted was also involved in the study and use of herbs as an alternative path. In addition to writing numerous books, he was a contributing author to various metaphysical magazines. He passed away in 2010.

How To

Heal with Color

Llewellyn Publications
Woodbury, Minnesota

SECOND EDITION
Fifth Printing, 2011

First edition, titled *How to Heal with Color,* eight printings.

Cover photograph © Koji Kitagawa/Superstock
Cover design by Gavin Dayton Duffy
Cover models used for illustrative purposes only and may not endorse or
    represent the book's subject.
Editing by Jennifer Gehlhar
Interior art by Llewellyn Art Department
Llewellyn is a registered trademark of Llewellyn Worldwide Ltd.

Library of Congress Cataloging-in-Publication Data
Andrews, Ted, 1952-2010
    How to heal with color / Ted Andrews.—2nd ed.
        p. cm. — (How to)
    Includes bibliographical references.
    ISBN 13: 978-0-7387-0811-9
    ISBN 10: 0-7387-0811-9 — ISBN 0-87542-005-2
  1. Color—Therapeutic use. 2. Color—Psychological aspects. I. Title.

    II. Series.

RZ414.6.A63 2006
615.8'312—dc22   2005047233

Llewellyn Worldwide does not participate in, endorse, or have any au-
thority or responsibility concerning private business transactions between our authors and the public.

    All mail addressed to the author is forwarded but the publisher cannot,
unless specifically instructed by the author, give out an address or phone
number.

    Any Internet references contained in this work are current at publi-
cation time, but the publisher cannot guarantee that a specific location
will continue to be maintained. Please refer to the publisher's website for
links to authors' websites and other sources.

    The information in this book is not intended to replace professional
medical advice. It is not prescriptive in any manner. Always consult a
qualified physician for any health problems.

Llewellyn Publications
A Division of Llewellyn Worldwide Ltd.
2143 Wooddale Drive
Woodbury, MN 55125-2989
www.llewellyn.com

Printed in the United States of America

Other Llewellyn Books by Ted Andrews

Contents

One

World of Light and Color

Everyone has an opinion on colors. Everyone has a favorite. Everyone is also affected by colors, often more than realized. Color is intimately tied to all aspects of our lives. It has even become a significant part of our language. We use colors to describe our physical health, emotions, attitudes, and even spiritual experiences. Listen to the conversations that people have; you can't help noticing how frequently color is used as part of our normal vocabulary:

"I'm in the pink today."

"You look at the world through rose-colored glasses."

"He was red with anger."

"His business was in the red last year, but now it is in the black."

"She has the blues today."

"They are all green with envy."

"It was a rich, golden experience."

"She has a yellow streak down her back."

No one is neutral when it comes to colors. There are always some colors we like more than others, and there are some we just do not like at all. Did you ever wonder why this is so? Did you ever wonder what this thing called color is and why it is so important to understand? Does color affect us more than we realize? Can colors be used to alter our physical, emotional, mental, and spiritual conditions? And if so, can we all learn to use them to enhance our lives? These questions and more will be answered throughout this text, as you learn to experience colors from a new level and learn to heal with them.

Let us begin with light. What is light? Light creates color and form. From a scientific point of view, light is electromagnetic energy that is produced by the sun in differing wavelengths. When these light waves bounce off objects and then hit our eyes, they create the sensation of light. Everything we see is created by reflected light. Low frequency light waves register in the brain as the color red. Violet is the result of high frequency light waves. Here is an experiment that shows you how light travels in the dark, but does not become visible until it reflects off of something.

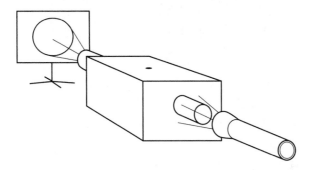

Proving We See by Reflected Light

Paint the inside of a cardboard box a flat black. Make a hole on each end, just large enough to fit half of a paper towel tube. Insert a tube into each end of the box, so that an inch to an inch and a half is inside each end. Then seal the box tightly, so that no light leaks through. Cut a tiny peephole in the top.

Shine a flashlight through one of the tubes. Hold a piece of paper near the other tube to make sure the light is passing through the box. As you do this, look through the peephole. The inside will be completely dark, even though the light is passing through and being reflected on the paper you are holding!

Next, allow a little smoke into the box. Once again, shine the light through one of the tubes. As you look into the peephole, you will see the beam of light passing through the box. This is because the light is now reflecting off the particles of smoke.

Due to the molecular structure and pigmentation of each object, light rays are mixed, absorbed, and reflected in varying speeds and intensities. Objects that appear to be dark absorb more light rays and thus reflect less light back to the eyes. This absorption creates the illusion of a deeper, darker color. Lighter objects reflect more light, giving the illusion of more brilliance and intensity.

Light waves change speed when they move from one kind of material into another. For example, light travels slower in water than in air: a pencil in a glass of water will appear to be broken; a hand submerged in water will appear larger. These visual changes occur because the light waves are bent as they move from air to water. (See The Speed of Light illustration.)

So, when do colors enter the equation? Well, when light is broken down (reflected and absorbed) into different wavelengths, we end up with different colors. It is like holding up a prism to the sunlight. It displays a rainbow on an opposite surface. (See The Prism illustration, page 6.) The seven colors of the rainbow are only a small fraction of the entire light spectrum. Each color has a multitude of shades and variations.

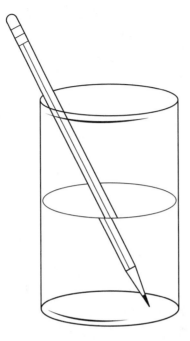

The Speed of Light

Light travels at slower speeds in water than in air. As a result, the reflected light is bent and can create variations and distortions.

Each color possesses its own absorptive and reflective properties. For example, when daylight strikes different colors, all of the light rays are absorbed and reflected according to the object. A yellow cloth will absorb all of the light rays, but it will separate the yellow wave and reflect it back out to the eyes. We see the cloth as yellow.

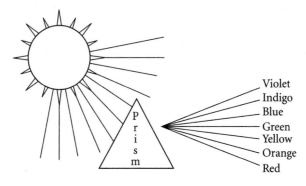

The Prism

As sunlight hits the prism, the prism breaks the light wave into the seven colors of the rainbow.

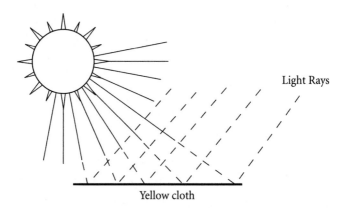

How We See Color

Cloth absorbs all of the rays except for the yellow frequency, which is reflected. We then see the cloth as yellow.

What does this have to do with healing? Very simply, the different frequencies of light (the colors) will affect different energies of the body. Some colors can more easily affect the higher frequencies of the brain because they have a higher light wave frequency. Other colors can affect bodily systems or energies that operate at slower rates because they have a lower frequency.

To fully understand this, we must begin to see ourselves as an energy system. Everything in life is formed from vibration. This vibration is the result of electron and proton movement in every atom of every molecule in every substance within the universe. Vibration exists in objects, animals, people, and the atmosphere surrounding us. The vibrational frequency of animate life is more active, vibrant, and variant than inanimate matter, but vibration exists in all things.

The human body has many energy fields. These energy fields surround, emanate from, and interact with the physical body and its various functions. These energy fields include, but are not limited to: light (colors), electricity, heat, sound, magnetism, and electromagnetism. They are scientifically measurable. One task of the modern metaphysical scientist is to determine which energies, intensities, and combinations are most effective in the healing process.

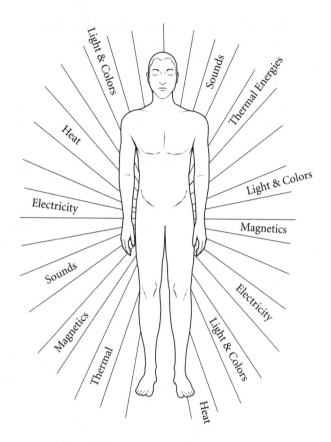

Energy Emanations of the Physical Body

All of the organs, tissues, and systems within our body have similar vibrating atoms. If something irritating—such as an improper food substance—enters the body, it can alter the normal vibrational pattern of the body—in this case, the digestive system. At these times, the body needs something to help restore its original vibrational pattern. In doing this, we can restore balance to problem areas.

Vibrational remedies are subtle energy stimuli that interact with the energy system of the human body to help stabilize physical, emotional, mental, and spiritual conditions. By providing the correct focus of energy to a problem area, we can temporarily restore balance to that area. Once balance is restored, we can more effectively rid ourselves of toxins, negativities, and patterns that hinder our life processes. Through vibrational remedies we revive a proper flow of energy. Some of the most effective vibrational remedies are sounds, aromas, flower and gem essences, crystals, stones, thoughts, and—of course!—color.

Two

Colors and Their Effects

Color can be used for healing and balancing, as well as for stimulating deeper levels of consciousness. Each color has its own unique effects, from stimulating to depressing, constructive to destructive.

The techniques throughout this book will assist you in working with the various colors and their shades so as to achieve the greatest effect in the healing process. Because each person has his or her own unique energy system, some experimentation is necessary to find the most beneficial color combination for each individual situation.

Colors are usually broken down into three categories. First, there are the primary colors of red, yellow, and blue. From a mixture of these three will come most of the other colors: secondary colors are formed from combinations of the primary colors; tertiary colors are formed by combinations of the primary and secondary colors.

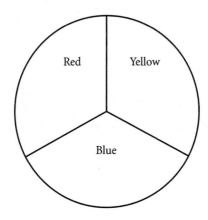

Primary Colors

The three primary colors are the foundation from which almost all other colors are derived.

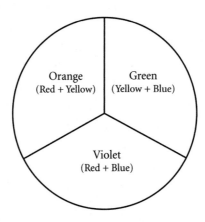

Secondary Colors

Secondary colors are formed by combining two of the primary colors: 50 percent of one primary color is added to 50 percent of another to form a new color.

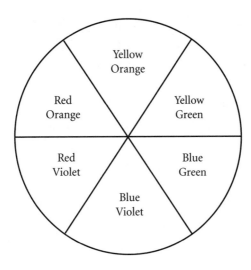

Tertiary Colors

The tertiary colors are formed by combining a primary color with a secondary color. As you learn to combine different colors and combinations, you begin to form the many shades within a particular color's spectrum.

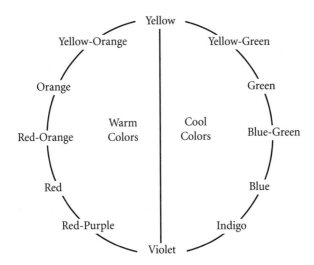

Colors from a Psychological Perspective

Working with colors in healing involves two steps. First, you must understand the individual properties of each color. Second, you must learn specific techniques to project and absorb color. To do this, you must become more color sensitive and knowledgeable. The more knowledgeable you become about colors, the easier it will be to balance and heal with them. There are several exercises to help you develop color sensitivity in chapter 2. Included is an exercise designed to teach you how to develop your innate ability to project color radiations through your hands. It is the first of many such exercises found throughout this book. But first we will familiarize ourselves with the many colors available to us.

The Meaning of Colors

I have assembled a list of color associations and uses. These are meant to be guidelines. They are not carved in stone. They are characteristics designed to help you begin your work with color therapy. You'll notice I included references to chakras. I will discuss chakras in greater detail in chapter 4. As you work with different individuals, you will discover that certain shades are more effective than others, depending upon the person. You may also discover that certain colors may not work for an individual's condition. In cases such as these, a little experimentation and a little intuition will help you discover the best colors to use for the best results. Remember that each individual has a unique energy system. Color combination and application must always be adapted to the individual.

White

White contains the entire light spectrum. It is strengthening. It is very cleansing and purifying to the entire energy system of the individual. It can awaken great creativity. When in doubt as to what color to use, you can seldom go wrong with white light. It is also beneficial to begin and end the healing session with white to stabilize the person's energy system and to give it an overall boost. It amplifies the effects of any color with which it is used.

Black

Black contains the entire color spectrum. It is a color that is shrouded in confusion. Many individuals shy away from using black in color therapy and healing, but I have found it beneficial at times. Black is a protective color, and it can be used to ground and calm extremely sensitive individuals. It activates the feminine or magnetic energies of the body, strengthening them. It should be used sparingly, as too much black can cause depression or aggravate such emotional and mental conditions.

Black is most effective when used in conjunction with white, which balances the polarities of the individual, especially in cases where the individual seems to be losing control. It can activate a level of the subconscious that puts life and its craziness into proper perspective. It should never be used by itself, but always in combination with another color.

Red

Red is a stimulating color. It warms and activates, energizing the base chakra and awakening our physical life force. Red strengthens the physical energy and the will of the individual. It can be used for colds and mucus ailments. Red can also be used to raise the body's temperature and to energize the blood, which helps in treating poor circulation. Red stimulates deeper passions, such as sex and love, hatred and revenge, and courage.

Too much red can overstimulate and aggravate conditions. High blood pressure is an indication of too much red energy within the system.

Orange

Orange is the color of joy and wisdom. It stimulates feelings of sociability. It is tied to our emotional health and to the muscular system of the body. Orange can assist in healing conditions of the spleen, pancreas, stomach, intestines, and adrenals. Individuals experiencing emotional paralysis or depression can be helped with this bright, uplifting color. It can be used to revitalize the physical body and assist with food assimilation. It makes a good tonic after a bout of illness, for it is good in eliminating negativity in the body.

Too much orange affects the nerves and should be balanced with shades of green-blues.

Yellow

Yellow is stimulating to the mental faculties. It affects the solar plexus chakra most strongly. It helps reawaken an enthusiasm for life, providing greater confidence and optimism. Therefore, it can be useful for treating depression. It can also be beneficial treatment for digestion problems. It helps balance the entire gastrointestinal tract—including the stomach, intestines, and bladder—and the entire eliminative system of the body. The golden-yellow shades are healthful to both the body and the mind.

Too much yellow may create nervousness and excessive thinking.

Green

Green is the most predominant color on the planet. It balances our energies, and it can be used to increase our sensitivity and compassion. It has a calming effect, especially for inflamed conditions of the body. It is soothing to the nervous system. The brighter greens, leaning toward the blue spectrum, are powerful in healing most conditions. Green can be used to awaken greater friendliness, hope, faith, and peace. It is restful and revitalizing to overtaxed mental conditions.

Green strongly affects the heart chakra, and it is balancing to the autonomic nervous system. It can be applied beneficially in cardiac conditions, high blood pressure, ulcers, exhaustion, and headaches.

It should *never* be used in cancerous or tumorous conditions or anything of a malignant nature, as green also stimulates growth.

Blue

Blue is cooling to our system and it is relaxing. Blue activates the throat chakra. It is quieting to our energies and it has an antiseptic effect as well. It is strengthening and balancing to the respiratory system of the body and all conditions of the throat. It is effective in easing childhood diseases, especially asthma, chickenpox, jaundice, and rheumatism. In fact, it is one of the most healing colors for children. It is beneficial to venous conditions of the body. Thus, it is excellent treatment for high blood pressure. Blue can also be used to awaken intuition and to ease loneliness. It is very effective when combined with warmer colors that are in its color range as well as colors in the red-orange spectrum. It can also be used to awaken artistic expression and inspiration.

Too much blue may result in procrastination, or may be too calming, hindering alertness.

Indigo

Indigo and the deeper shades of blue are dynamic healing colors on both spiritual and physical levels. This color activates the brow chakra of the body and it is balancing to all conditions associated with it. It is strengthening to the lymph system, glands, and immune system. It is an excellent blood purifier and can assist in detoxifying the body. It is a color that is balancing to the hemispheres of the brain and the nerve synapses between them. It is effective in treating all conditions of the face, including eyes, ears, nose, mouth, and sinuses.

The color indigo also has a sedative effect. You can use the color indigo to achieve deeper levels of consciousness when you are meditating. It can awaken devotion and intuition. It can also be used for problems in the lungs and for removing certain obsessions.

Too much indigo can cause depression and a sense of separateness from others.

Violet

Violet is a color that affects the skeletal system of the body. It activates the crown chakra. It is very antiseptic, cleansing, and purifying on physical and spiritual levels. It helps balance the physical and the spiritual energies. Violet is good to use for cancerous conditions of the "body." Arthritis can be eased by violet light that leans more toward the blue shades. Violet is also strengthening to the body's ability to assimilate and use minerals. It can be used to stimulate inspiration and humility. Violet assists in stimulating dream activity as well. In meditation, violet can help open us to our past lives.

Too much violet may lead to depression, and it can bring old issues to the surface at inappropriate times.

Pink

Pink can be used to awaken compassion, love, and purity. It eases conditions of anger and feelings of neglect. It helps stimulate the thymus gland and the immune system of the body. It can be used in meditation to discern greater truths. Pink is comforting to the emotional energies of the individual.

Too much pink may make you hypersensitive and emotional.

Lemon

Lemon is vitalizing and stimulating to the brain. It contains a shade of green within its spectrum, and this works as a cleanser.

Too much lemon has the same effects as too much yellow.

Purple

Purple is purifying to the system. It can be used to stimulate venous activity in the body. It can also be used for headaches. The red-purple range is beneficial for balancing polarities of the body; the blue-purple range can often be used effectively to shrink things (as in the case of tumors) and to cool the skin, easing inflammation.

Because of its high vibration, purple should be used sparingly: too much purple can create or aggravate depression.

Silver

Silver and some grays can be used to amplify the effects of other colors, much in the manner of white. Silver is effective in meditations used to discover the metaphysical source of an illness or disease. And it is wise to remember that unless we discover the source of an illness, the likelihood of its recurrence is high. It can also be used to help an individual discover and apply their own creative imagination. It activates innate intuition.

Too much silver may create over-reliance on intuition with no regard for logic or common sense.

Brown

Brown is also a color that can be used in healing. It is especially effective for emotional and mental conditions. Brown can help awaken common sense and discrimination. It can help bring an individual "back down to earth." It is effective for eliminating that spacey feeling.

Too much brown may make an individual very materialistic and stimulate greediness—feelings of "not having enough."

Common Ailments and Beneficial Colors

This next list is only a guideline; it is *not* prescriptive. Like the last reference list, this is a set of suggestions to help you find a starting point for working with color therapy. It is not designed to replace traditional medicine; rather, it is intended to provide a means by which you can participate more personally in your own healing process. Use it as such, so that you can develop your own system of color application. Eventually, you'll find what works best for you. You may need to apply different colors with different intensities. Often, experimentation is the only way to discover what works.

I suggest you begin all color treatments with white and end them with white. This amplifies the treatments' effects, and it serves to keep the color treatments from aggravating a condition: it provides balance. Remember that the red spectrum affects the physical, and is stimulating and warming. Blues are cooling and cleansing, affecting the spiritual energies. The yellow shades affect the mental energies and serve as a bridge between the physical and spiritual.

The three together—reds, blues, and yellows—provide opportunities for healing body, spirit, and mind.

Conditions and Corresponding Colors

Condition	*Beneficial Colors*
Abdominal Cramps	Yellow, Lemon
Abscesses	Blue, Blue-Violet
Aches (ear)	Turquoise
Aches (head)	Blue, Green
Aches (muscles)	Pastel Orange
Aches (tooth)	Blue, Blue-Violet
Acne	Red, Red-Violet
AIDS	Red, Indigo, or Violet followed by Pink and Gold
Alcoholism	Indigo and Yellow
Allergies	Indigo and Soft Orange
Alzheimer's Disease	Royal Blue or Blue-Purple followed by Yellow

Condition	*Beneficial Colors*
Anemia	Red
Anxieties	Light Blue and Green
Appetite (excessive)	Indigo
Appetite (loss)	Yellow, Lemon
Arthritis	Violet, Blue-Violet, or Red-Violet
Asthma	Blue and Orange
Bladder	Yellow-Orange
Bleeding	Blue-Green
Blisters	Powder or Ice Blue
Blood Pressure (high)	Blue, Green
Blood Pressure (low)	Red, Red-Orange
Bones	Violet, Lemon
Bowels	Yellow-Orange
Breast	Pink, Red-Violet
Bronchitis	Blue, Blue-Green, Turquoise
Burns	Blue, Blue-Green
Burping	Yellow, Lemon
Cancer	Blue or Blue-Violet followed by Pink
Colds	Reds
Diabetes	Violet
Eczema	Lemon
Epilepsy	Turquoise, Deep Blue

Condition	*Beneficial Colors*
Eyes	Indigo, Royal Blue
Fevers	Blue
Growths	Violet, Blue-Violet
Hay Fever	Red-Orange
Heart Problems	Green and Pink
Hemorrhoids	Deep Blue
Indigestion	Yellow, Lemon
Infection	Violet
Inflammation	Blue
Influenza	Deep Blue, Turquoise, Violet
Kidneys	Yellow, Yellow-Orange
Leukemia	Violet
Liver	Blue and Yellow combinations
Menstrual Problems	Soft Red with Blue-Green combinations
Nausea	Ice Blue
Nerves	Green, Blue-Green
Parkinson's	Indigo
Pneumonia	Red or Red-Orange, combined with Indigo
Rash	Lemon and Turquoise
Skin Problems	Lemon, Blue-Violet
Swelling	Pale and Ice Blues
Ulcers	Green

Three

Developing Color Sensitivity

We are all sensitive to color. We know which colors we like. We also know which colors we dislike. We can tell, even if we can't define why, when a color is not "right" for someone. Color and light do affect us. The more sensitive we can become to color and its effects, the more we can use it to our benefit.

One of the easiest ways to develop greater color sensitivity and knowledge is through color flashcards. Simply get a set of 3 x 5 index cards. On one side of the card, list the various attributes of a specific color. On the opposite side, use markers or crayons to color it appropriately. Have one card for every color. Begin with the seven colors of the rainbow. Once you make the flashcards, you can try this exercise:

Relax your mind. Perform a progressive relaxation or some rhythmic breathing. Take a moment or two to study the cards one at a time. Focus on the color, then read the characteristics to yourself. Go through all of the colors several times.

The next step is to become sensitive to how the colors feel. Our hands have the capability of sensing energy changes and differences. We have all experienced some aspects of this. When we touch someone or shake his or her hand, we get impressions about that person. Our hands—our sense of touch—help us attune to that individual's energy. We can apply this innate ability to developing color sensitivity. Try this exercise:

With eyes closed, shuffle and mix the colored cards. Make sure the colored surfaces of your index cards are facing up. Pulling one from the set, hold your hand over it. Stay relaxed. Allow your hand to do the sensing. Begin by trying to determine if it has a warm feel or a cool feel. This lets you know whether it is in the red (warm) spectrum or the blue (cool) spectrum.

What else do you feel or sense as you hold your hand over the color? Do you think you know what color it may be? Is there any kind of tingling? Do you notice anything in any particular part of your body? Pay attention to every impression—no matter how odd it may seem. These little details will eventually help you become more knowledgeable about the color and its possible effects and applications.

With practice, you will develop the ability to identify the color by its feel. Remember, you are working with subtle vibrational energies; and you are working to develop your sensitivity to those subtle energy fields surrounding you. With further practice, you will not only be able to sense colors with your hands, you will also be able to project color energies with them.

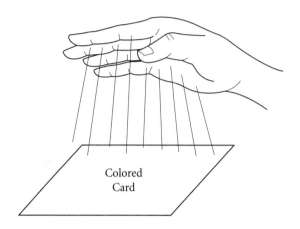

Developing a Sensitivity to Color Through Touch

Color Therapy Through Touch

In this next exercise we learn that we can project energies using thought and our own hands. An old occult axiom teaches that all energy follows thought. Where we put our thoughts is where our energy goes. For example, if we focus on a color, the energy emanations from the body begin to change to a frequency that resonates with that particular color.

Energy emanates more strongly from the hands than from other parts of the body; thus, hands can be used to sense and project subtle energy. It is this projection of healing energy that is often known as laying on of hands, therapeutic touch, etheric healing, or the King's Touch.

Begin this exercise by rubbing the palms of your hands together for about fifteen to thirty seconds. This activates the chakras in the palms and increases their sensitivity. Extend your hands in front of you, holding them about a foot apart. Slowly bring the palms toward each other. Bring them as close to each other as you can without touching them. Then, slowly draw them apart, to about six inches. Repeat this in and out movement. Keep your movements slow and steady.

As you perform this exercise, pay attention to what you feel or sense. You may feel warmth or coolness. You may experience a feeling of pressure building up. It may seem as if the space between your hands is thickening. There may be a sense of tickling or pressure; you may even experience a pulsating feeling.

Take a few minutes to try and define what you are feeling. Do not worry whether you are imagining it or not. Do not worry that it may feel different from how others may experience it. It is important to define what you sense or feel for yourself. This exercise develops concentration, and it helps to confirm that our energy field does not stop at skin level. It also helps you to define your own energy radiations.

The in and out movement of the hands causes the energy surrounding them to accumulate, making it more perceptible to us.

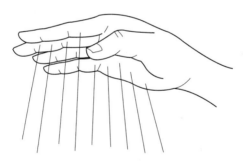

With practice, we can control the intensity and flow of this energy through our hands by focusing the mind on a specific color.

Color Therapy Through Touch

The next step is to learn that you can control the intensity of the energy radiations from your hands. This can be most easily accomplished with an everyday outdoor thermometer. Begin by making yourself comfortable and relaxed. Again, briskly rub the palms of your hands together to activate the chakras in them. Take the thermometer and place it between your hands. You may either hold it in your hands or stand it up, so that your hands are two to three inches from either side of it.

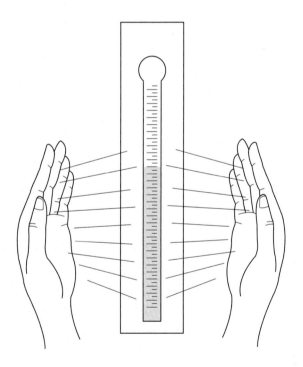

Changing the Temperature

As we learn to radiate energy through our hands, we can change temperature by color—red to warm something, blue to cool it.

Begin to do some slow, rhythmic breathing. As you breathe in slowly, see and feel your body filling with warm, bright red energy. As you exhale, see and feel this energy pouring out of your hands, toward the thermometer. Visualize, sense, and project heat—red heat—from your hands onto the thermometer. See how much you can raise the temperature in three to five minutes.

Now try using cool colors. Begin to feel and see your body filling with cool, blue energy with each inhalation. As you exhale, visualize this energy pouring out of your hands to lower the temperature of the thermometer. See, feel, and imagine your hands projecting icy energy in the form of the color blue, onto the thermometer. See how much you can lower the temperature in three to five minutes.

Have fun with this exercise! It shows you that you can change energy emanations from your hands by your thoughts. You are learning to project colors, developing a rainbow healing touch.

Healing a Headache with a Touch of Color

One of the most common ailments is the headache. It is also one of the simplest to eliminate through color. Most headaches are the result of an overstimulation of the brow or crown chakra. It is almost as if they become slightly inflamed. Cooling those centers down serves to alleviate the problem.

We learned in the previous exercise that we can project energy through our hands at a frequency associated with the color upon which we are focusing. We simply apply this energy to the headache. For most headaches a soft, cool blue or blue-green combination is most beneficial. For deeper seated pains, such as in the case of migraines, indigo is the most soothing. This next example explains how you can treat another person's headache:

1. Take a few moments to relax yourself.

2. Begin rhythmic breathing. As you breathe in, feel the blue energy building in your body and moving toward your hands.

3. Have the person with the headache sit down in front of you. Instruct him or her to gently close the eyes and relax.

4. Place your hands two to three inches from the front and back of the individual's head. (See Healing a Headache with Color illustration.) If you wish, you can lay your hands directly on the person's head.

5. Continue your breathing. As you exhale, see and feel this cool, blue energy filling the head of the person, balancing, calming, and soothing the pain. Picture the blue as a colored aspirin if it helps. You may wish to move the hands to the sides of the head, where the temples are located. Noticeable results usually occur in less than five minutes.

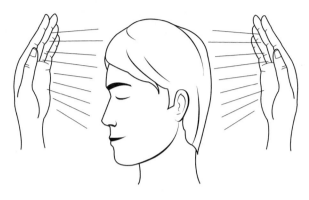

Healing a Headache with Color

All energy follows thought. As we concentrate the mind on a particular color, a signal is sent to the energy that is being projected from the hands. The color we focus on determines the vibration of that projection. We can use our hands to heal or alleviate conditions through simple touch.

If you wish to heal yourself, merely place the hands over your temple, followed by placing one hand on your forehead and the other on the back of your head. Visualize the color yellow streaming through your hands.

Four

Color Therapy for the Chakras

Because the human body is an energy system, we can use different energy forms to interact with the functions of that system. Understanding the human chakra system is the key to understanding how to use color as a part of the healing process. The word *chakra* is Sanskrit, and it means "wheel."

Chakras are the primary mediators of all energy coming into and radiating out of the body. In other words, they mediate the impulses of our energy system. Although not part of the physical body, they link the subtle energy fields surrounding the body to the activities of the body itself. This is often thought of as metaphysical "mumbo jumbo," but modern science has shown that in the areas of the body where chakras are traditionally located, the electromagnetic emanations are higher.

Chakras help the body distribute energy for its various physical, emotional, mental, and spiritual functions.

Each chakra is connected to functions of the physical body, primarily through the endocrine glands and spinal system. Chakras mediate energy inside and outside of the body through the various spinal contacts. This energy is distributed throughout the body by means of the nerve pathways and the circulatory system. In this way, all of the organs, tissues, and cells receive the vibrational energy accordingly.

One of the most effective means of restoring balance is through the use of color. Individual chakras and the related organs and systems in the body will respond to specific colors. If there is an imbalance, we can use colors or combinations of colors to restore homeostasis (balance) to a chakra and, thus, to those systems and energies of the body mediated by that chakra. This works because the color vibrations interact with the electromagnetic emanations of the body; more specifically, color vibrations are transmitted to the vertebrae of the spine, where the vertebrae transfer the color frequencies along the nerve pathways to the organs and systems of the body, restoring balance. This applies also to those emotional and mental imbalances that can cause or aggravate physical problems.

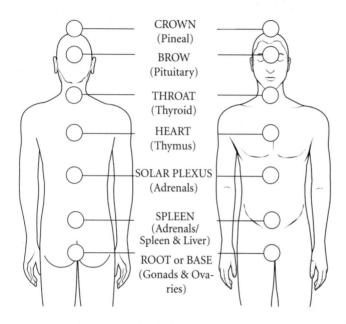

CROWN
(Pineal)

BROW
(Pituitary)

THROAT
(Thyroid)

HEART
(Thymus)

SOLAR PLEXUS
(Adrenals)

SPLEEN
(Adrenals/
Spleen & Liver)

ROOT or BASE
(Gonads & Ova-
ries)

The Chakra System

The chakras help distribute energy for our physical, emotional, mental, and spiritual functions. The seven major chakras are points of greater electromagnetic activity within the auric field. The hands and feet are other points of great activity. The subtle auric energies are more easily detectable around them.

The most confusing aspect of working with colors is deciding which color(s) will be most beneficial. Often this can be a trial and error process, but there are ways of eliminating much of the trial. With a basic knowledge of chakras and their health correspondences, we can more easily discern the color therapy most beneficial for us.

What follows in the rest of this chapter is a brief examination of the chakra system and its links to our health. This is followed by a method to assess the ailing chakra in order to determine its color therapy. To conclude, a simple chakra color healing technique is provided for you.

Base Chakra: Red

Color Application

If underactive, use red; if overactive, use green followed by a small dose of red.

Physical Functions

This chakra is located in the area of the coccyx (at the base of the spine). It is tied to the functions of the circulatory system, reproductive system, and the lower extremities. It is the center for our basic life force. It influences the testicles and ovaries, legs, feet, and pelvic area.

Metaphysical Functions

This is a center tied to that level of consciousness that controls our life-promoting energies. Stimulated properly, it can awaken awareness of past-life talents and ease fears.

Emotional / Mental Attitudes Causing or Reflecting Dysfunction

Overactive Base Chakra

Physically aggressive, belligerent, impulsive, inability to recognize limits, obsessively sexual, hyperactive, reckless.

Underactive Base Chakra

Manipulative, overly cautious, power conscious, possessive, needing approval, craving excitement and change but refusing to act upon it, overly tired, no energy to do what you want. Reactiveness, aggression, belligerence, manipulative.

Spleen Chakra: Orange

Color Application

If underactive, apply orange; if overactive, use blue followed by a small dose of orange.

Physical Functions

This center is partially tied to the functions of the adrenal glands. It is also a major influence on the reproductive system and the entire muscular system. It affects the eliminative system of the body, and the activities of the spleen, bladder, pancreas, and kidneys. It is a major center for detoxifying the body.

Metaphysical Functions

This center influences sensation, emotion, desire, pleasure, and sexuality. It is linked to the consciousness of creativity. It controls many personality functions. It can be stimulated with color to open communication with energies and beings upon the astral plane of life.

Emotional / Mental Attitudes Causing or Reflecting Dysfunction

Overactive Spleen Chakra

Selfish, arrogant, lustful, overly proud or conceited, emotionally high-strung, constantly power-seeking.

Underactive Spleen Chakra

Mistrust others, introverted, unable to show emotions, worrying what others think, antisocial, follow the crowd.

Solar Plexus Chakra: Yellow

Color Application

If underactive, use yellow; if overactive, use violet or purple, with a small dose of yellow.

Physical Functions

This chakra is tied to the solar plexus area of the body. This includes the digestive system, adrenals, stomach, liver, and gallbladder. It assists the body in assimilation of nutrients. It is also tied to functions of the left hemisphere of the brain. Many crippling diseases, ulcers, intestinal problems, and psychosomatic diseases are eased by working with this center.

Metaphysical Functions

This center is tied to the level of consciousness that can make us clairsentient (the ability to sense the feelings and emotions of others). It is a center of empathy and general psychic impressions. When stimulated, it opens awareness of the talents and capacities of other souls. It helps attune us to the elements of nature.

Emotional / Mental Attitudes Causing or Reflecting Dysfunction

Overactive Solar Plexus Chakra

Judgmental and critical, mentally bullying, absolutist in attitude, always planning and never manifesting, stubborn, needing constant change/variety.

Underactive Solar Plexus Chakra

Feeling deprived of recognition, aloof, feeling isolated, afraid to learn the new, psychosomatic problems.

Heart Chakra: Green

Color Application

If underactive, use green; if overactive, use green followed by pink or soft reds.

Physical Functions

This center is influential in the functions, of the thymus gland and the entire immune system of the body. It is tied to the heart and the pulmonary activities, along with the circulatory system. It affects the assimilation of nutrients. It has a powerful influence on childhood diseases and the development of a strong immune system from them. It also has ties to activities of tissue regeneration.

Metaphysical Functions

This center mediates and balances activities of other chakras. If it is out of balance, there is likely to be imbalance in the others. It is tied to that level of our consciousness that awakens higher compassion and our innate healing abilities. If stimulated properly with color, it can open an ability to see the deeper forces in plants and animals, along with a knowledge of the sentiments and true dispositions of others.

Emotional / Mental Attitudes Causing or Reflecting Dysfunction

Overactive Heart Chakra

Angry, jealous, blaming others, miserly and stingy, overconfident, allowing oneself to be walked on and taken advantage of.

Underactive Heart Chakra

Needing constant confirmation of self-worth, uncertain, unable to enforce will, possessive, self-doubting, feeling unloved, lacking compassion.

Throat Chakra: Blue

Color Application

If underactive, use blue; if overactive, use orange followed by a small dose of blue.

Physical Functions

The throat chakra is tied to the functions of the throat, esophagus, mouth, teeth, thyroid, and parathyroid glands. It strongly affects the respiratory system, the functions of the bronchia, and the entire vocal apparatus.

Metaphysical Functions

This chakra is tied to functions of the right hemisphere of the brain and the creative functions of the mind. It can be stimulated with color to awaken clairaudience (hearing spirit) and to assist us in manifesting greater abundance. It can also be stimulated to awaken telepathy (so as to survey the thoughts of others). And it can awaken our level of consciousness that has insight into the true laws of natural phenomena.

Emotional / Mental Attitudes Causing or Reflecting Dysfunction

Overactive Throat Chakra

Domineering, dogmatic, fanatical, over-reacting, speaks negatively/harshly, clings to tradition, hyperactive.

Underactive Throat Chakra

Surrenders to others, resists change, melancholy, slow to respond, stubborn.

Brow Chakra: Indigo

Color Application

If underactive, use indigo; if overactive, use soft orange or peach followed by a small dose of indigo.

Physical Functions

The brow center influences the functions of the pituitary gland and the entire endocrine system. It also has links to the immune system. It affects the synapses of the brain, and it is key to balanced operation of the hemispheres of the brain. It affects the sinuses, eyes, ears, and entire face in general.

Metaphysical Functions

This is the center affecting higher clairvoyance and the entire magnetism of the body (the feminine aspects of our energies). It is linked to that level of the subconscious mind that controls intuitive perceptions, creative imagination, and visualization.

Emotional / Mental Attitudes Causing or Reflecting Dysfunction

Overactive Brow Chakra

Worrying, fearful, oversensitive, impatient, belittling the behaviors of others, "spaced out."

Underactive Crown Chakra

Doubting, envious of others' talents, forgetful, superstitious, fearful, worrying.

Crown Chakra: Violet

Color Application

If underactive, use violet; if overactive, use yellow followed by a small dose of violet.

Physical Functions

This center affects the functions of the entire nervous system and the entire skeletal system of the body. It influences the pineal gland, all nerve pathways, and the electrical synapses within the body. It is linked to the proper function of the medulla oblongata.

Metaphysical Functions

This chakra is a link to that level of the subconscious mind that has ties to our most spiritual essence. It is a center that helps to align us with the higher forces of the universe, and it has a powerful influence in the purification of our subtle bodies of energy. This center is a link to past lives and their effects upon us in the present.

Emotional / Mental Attitudes Causing or Reflecting Dysfunction

Overactive Crown Chakra

Intensely erotic imagination, needing to feel popular and indispensable, needing sympathy.

Underactive Crown Chakra

Feeling misunderstood, shame, self-denial, negative self-image, lacking tenderness.

Chakra Assessment

The ancient masters taught their students to be ever watchful. This meant paying attention to the various emotions and attitudes that they experienced or were exposed to throughout the day. As they did this, they could then determine which chakra center(s) was most likely to be unbalanced. They would then take extra care to balance those centers at the end of the day. In this manner, the imbalance did not have a chance to accumulate, ultimately causing or aggravating a physical problem. We can do the same thing.

We have just examined the chakra system of the body. We now understand how the various physical systems and organs of the body are affected by the chakras and how emotional and mental attitudes can aggravate

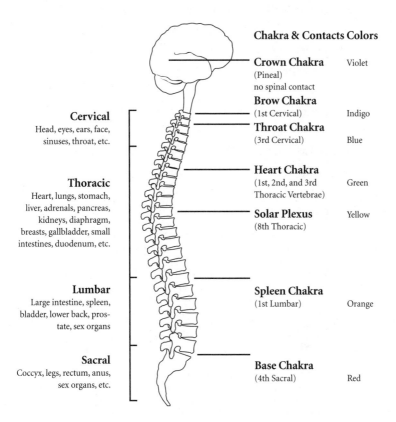

Chakra & Contacts Colors

Crown Chakra (Pineal) no spinal contact	Violet	
Brow Chakra (1st Cervical)	Indigo	
Throat Chakra (3rd Cervical)	Blue	
Heart Chakra (1st, 2nd, and 3rd Thoracic Vertebrae)	Green	
Solar Plexus (8th Thoracic)	Yellow	
Spleen Chakra (1st Lumbar)	Orange	
Base Chakra (4th Sacral)	Red	

Cervical
Head, eyes, ears, face, sinuses, throat, etc.

Thoracic
Heart, lungs, stomach, liver, adrenals, pancreas, kidneys, diaphragm, breasts, gallbladder, small intestines, duodenum, etc.

Lumbar
Large intestine, spleen, bladder, lower back, prostate, sex organs

Sacral
Coccyx, legs, rectum, anus, sex organs, etc.

Spinal Contacts of the Chakras

Color vibrations enter through the chakras. They balance the chakras and are transmitted to the vertebrae of the spine. The vertebrae transfer these along the nerve pathways to the various organs and systems to which they are linked. Balance is restored.

or create dysfunction in the chakras and their corresponding physical elements. We also listed the colors primarily associated with the chakras.

With this knowledge behind us, we are now ready to do the chakra assessment technique. In this assessment, we examine the problem area and determine which chakra is most likely to be unbalanced. Usually the chakra associated with a particular problem will be overactive or underactive.

As you now know, there are specific colors that are useful to balance chakras. We can use these specific colors to help balance chakras, thus easing physical, emotional, mental, or even spiritual problems.

An underactive chakra is usually one in which the energy is congested. If congested, energy does not flow freely through the chakra and its physical systems. A congested base chakra, for example, may reflect itself in physical conditions such as tiredness, anemia, etc. Keep in mind that this is the center for our basic life force. If it is congested or underactive, we just do not have enough energy to perform our functions during the day. An application of the color red can help stimulate the base chakra into greater activity.

An overactive chakra is one in which too much energy is being drawn in and out of a particular center, aggravating a specific condition. In other words, the chakra is inflamed. For example, an overactive base chakra may reflect itself through high blood pressure and even belligerence and aggression. The color green, as indicated for in chapter 2, will calm and soothe the chakra.

A general rule of thumb for the chakras is as follows: An underactive chakra can be treated with a strong dose of its basic color. An overactive chakra is best treated by using its opposite color. To know which colors are opposite, refer to the Opposite Colors chart. If in doubt, apply

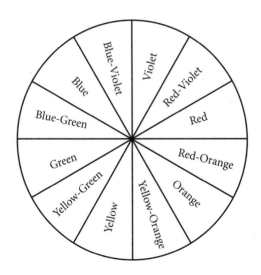

Opposite Colors

When we determine that a chakra is unbalanced, we then must decide whether it is overactive or underactive. If it is underactive, we simply apply the basic color of that chakra center. If it is an overactive chakra, we apply its opposite color to restore balance to it.

varying amounts of both colors to the chakra center. The opposite colors balance each other.

Simply follow these basic steps in this process:

1. Determine which chakra(s) is most likely out of balance. The physical condition and various emotional and mental attitudes will assist you in pinpointing the center. Use the chart in chapter 2 (see pages 22–24) and the correspondence guide in this chapter to assist you.

2. Determine if the chakra is overactive or under-active. If underactive, the energy and operation of physical systems involved will seem congested and slow; overactive is usually reflected by in-flammation, agitation, and hypersensitivity.

3. Apply the color therapy. You can use the meth-ods described at the end of this chapter or any combination of methods described throughout the book. The length of the color treatment will vary. In many cases you will have to use your in-tuition. Five to ten minutes per color is effective. You may wish to use the techniques described in the next chapter to assist you in determining the length of the treatment.

4. After applying color for the specific chakra, it is beneficial to follow it with a general balancing of all seven chakra centers. Do a quick ten- to fifteen-second color treatment for each chakra center, from the base to the crown. This further stabilizes your system.

Color Therapy for the Chakras

We can use color therapy to balance ourselves every day. In this way, we keep ourselves stronger, more balanced, and more vibrant. Any of the color application methods throughout the book can be used for this daily balancing. One of the easiest ways to accomplish this balancing is with simple color swatches that can be bought for two to three dollars at any fabric store. Most fabric stores sell felt or other cloth squares for about twenty cents a piece. They can be found in all of the colors of the rainbow as well as in other shades. Once you have purchased them, you can begin to balance your chakras. The following exercise may be used to heal yourself or others. I will explain the process as if you are healing yourself. When healing another person, you can read the steps aloud to him or her.

1. Make sure you will be undisturbed for about ten to fifteen minutes. It will rarely take any longer. Make sure the phone is off the hook, etc.

2. Lie down on your back—either on the floor or on your bed. Have your seven cloth swatches with you (red, orange, yellow, green, blue, indigo, and violet).

3. Close your eyes and relax. Take several deep breaths. As you begin to relax, look back over the day, in reverse order. When we look at the day in reverse order, we concentrate more, and we are less likely to skip over events and situations. Start with the moment you just laid down

for this healing session, and look back over the events of the day—all the way back to when you first got out of bed.

4. Note the major emotions and attitudes that you experienced and were exposed to throughout the day. What chakras were most likely to have been affected by them?

5. When you have completed your evaluation, take the color swatches for those chakras you have just identified, and lay them on the different corresponding parts of your body.

6. As you lie there with the color swatches upon your chakra points, visualize the colors being absorbed and drawn into your body. Know that as you lie there the chakras are balanced by the colors. Take several deep breaths, focusing on each chakra and drawing the color from the cloth swatch into your body to restore balance. Continue this for three to five minutes, or until you feel they are balanced.

7. Now place all seven color swatches upon the chakra points of the body, as shown in the Chakra Color Therapy illustration on page 54. Breathe deeply and allow your body to absorb the rainbow energies. Know that the colors are aligning and strengthening your chakras. Feel yourself balancing. Know that all of the physiological as-

pects of your body are being balanced and healed as you absorb these colors through your chakra centers. Leave the swatches on for three to five minutes, or until you feel fully balanced, charged, and aligned.

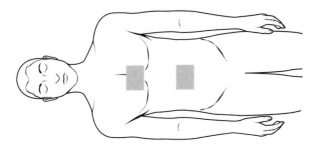

Begin by laying the colored cloth pieces upon the chakras you determined were most likely to be unbalanced.

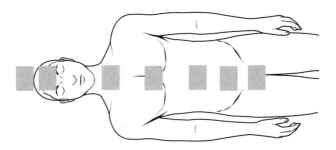

Next, lay the colored cloth swatches on each of the seven major chakras. Make sure you use the appropriate color for each center. Allow your body to absorb the energy for several minutes.

Chakra Color Therapy

Five

Determining the Colors Needed

The most confusing aspect of working with colors is deciding which color(s) will be the most beneficial. Often this can be a trial and error process, but there are ways of eliminating much of the trial.

We examined one such method in the last chapter: chakra assessment takes note of different conditions (physical or otherwise) that are relevant at the time, and with this information we can determine which colors to use in treatment. We will explore two more methods of color determination in this chapter. You do not have to use these techniques independently; all of them can be used separately or in combination. In all three methods, we are simply working to identify the subtle influences affecting us. It is in this way that we can more specifically determine the most beneficial color therapy.

Determining Color Therapy
Through Radiesthesia

Radiesthesia is a method of dowsing or divining to determine energy radiation. Our nervous system responds to subtle energies that we often do not consciously recognize. Radiesthesia involves using a tool to translate those unrecognized energies into something more tangible. The two most common tools of radiesthesia are the dowsing rod and the pendulum.

Any tool of radiesthesia has capabilities that go beyond mere healing. You can use radiesthesia tools to facilitate access to the subconscious mind. They can be used to awaken and activate your own psychic and intuitive feelings, to uncover past lives, to establish links with higher levels of knowledge, and to determine dream meanings. The pendulum and the dowsing rod have many applications. I highly recommend them for all who are involved in metaphysics.

The pendulum is particularly effective in helping us to determine appropriate colors (and their combinations) for therapy. It is a tool for communicating with the subconscious mind. For example, your subconscious is aware of every energy inside and outside your body; through the pendulum, you can expand your conscious perception by tapping into this subconscious bank of knowledge.

The pendulum gives no answer itself. The subconscious mind communicates to us through the nervous system. The nervous system translates the communication to an electrical signal and impulse, which then causes the pendulum to move. The swinging of the pendulum is an ideomotor response. It is caused by involuntary muscle action stimulated by the subconscious mind, which is cued by the sympathetic nervous system of the body.

Pendulums can be made from simple objects found around the home; just make sure the object used as a weight is heavy enough to swing, and that it is able to hang freely. There are four types of common pendulums. (See the Common Types of Pendulums illustration on the next page.)

The first step to using a pendulum is to get the feel of it. Take a seated position at a desk or table. Place your feet flat on the floor, resting your elbow on the desk. Hold the pendulum by the end of the chain between your thumb and index finger. Allow it to hang for a moment or two. Now circle it gently in a clockwise direction. Allow it to stop; then rotate it in a counterclockwise direction. Next, move it vertically, horizontally, and diagonally. Become comfortable with its feel.

The next step is to teach the pendulum how to respond to the subconscious mind. It is like programming your computer. You are telling it what kind of feedback you expect, so that you will be able to understand its movement when you ask it questions. Draw similar figures on a piece of paper and lay it on the desk, dangling the pendulum over its middle. (See Programming Pendulum Movements, page 60.)

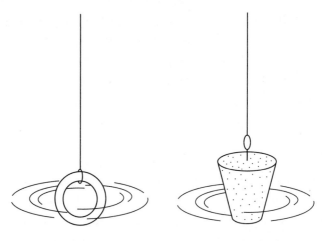

Simple ring on a string   A cork, needle, and thread

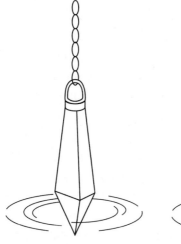

Quartz crystal pendulum   Common cross-and-chain necklace

Common Types of Pendulums

Tell yourself out loud, "When I ask a question and the answer is 'yes,' my subconscious will make the pendulum move in this direction: _____." Voice the coordinates you wish to work with—right, left, up, down, north, south, circular clockwise, etc.—as you simultaneously swing the pendulum in the same manner. For example, you could follow the method illustrated on page 60, in which case "yes" corresponds to the vertical axis. You would then swing your pendulum gently in the vertical line. You are simply programming the subconscious mind to move the pendulum in a consistent, recognizable manner when responding to your questions.

As you begin to program your pendulum, test it. Prove to yourself that it works. Rest your elbow comfortably and let the pendulum hang still. Think to yourself the word "yes." Repeat it in your mind and let your eyes look up and down the "yes" line. Do this until the pendulum swings up and down on its own. Stay relaxed. Now think to yourself, *Stop.* As the pendulum comes to a rest, repeat the procedure using the "no" line.

Once you become comfortable with the pendulum and its operation, you can use it to ask your subconscious and intuitive self what color(s) may be needed in any given situation. Construct a small chart that has a list of colors (see Determining Colors with a Pendulum, page 62). Hanging the pendulum over each color, ask the question, "Does _____ need this color?" (Insert your name or the name of someone with whom you are doing a healing.) If the pendulum answers "yes," pay attention

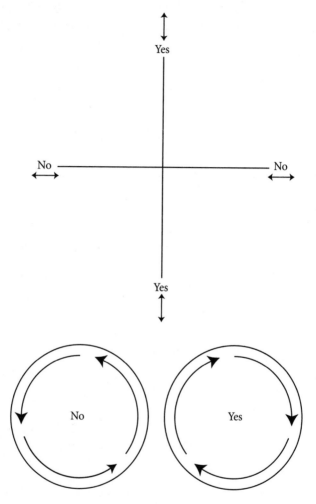

Programming Pendulum Movements

to the strength of the movement. The intensity and speed indicate how much of that particular color is needed. The faster the movement, the more of that color you "need."

Go through each of the colors on the chart with your pendulum. Make sure you phrase your question so that it can be answered with a simple "yes" or "no." Then, proceed to apply the suggested color treatment through any of the ways discussed in this book.

After the treatment, you may wish to check and see if more treatment is necessary. Ask your pendulum such questions as: "Does _____ need more red?" "Is five minutes enough time for treatment?" With practice, you will learn to use the pendulum to test and verify the effects of your color treatments with great accuracy.

Determining Color Therapy Through Kinesiology

Kinesiology is the study of muscle movements in the body—voluntary and involuntary—and their interactions with the rest of our energy system. Part of the study of kinesiology involves the connection between muscles and the electrical system of the body. As the muscles move, contracting and extending, electrical energy is released. If muscles are overworked, too much electrical energy is released, and soreness, weakness, and tiredness can result. If muscles are not worked enough, too much magnetic energy accumulates, resulting in softer muscle tissue and the accumulation of fat around the muscles.

Red	Red-Orange	Orange	Yellow-Orange	Yellow	Yellow-Green	Green	Blue-Green	Blue	Blue-Violet	Indigo	Violet	Red-Violet	Purple	White	Silver	Black

Determining Colors with a Pendulum

Once you are comfortable with the pendulum, use a color chart to help you determine the color(s) most beneficial for therapy and health. Allow the pendulum to hang freely over each color in turn, asking the question, "Is this color needed?" The pendulum movement will let you know the answer. After the treatment, you can go back and check the colors once more, simply by using the yes/no questioning approach. "Is more red needed?" "Does __ need more violet?" The pendulum is helping you access your intuitive mind so that the color can be applied more beneficially.

Our thoughts and emotions elicit specific brainwave pattern electromagnetic frequencies that can easily interfere with the functioning of our muscles and the entire electrical system of the body. This is why, in chapter 4, we outlined specific emotional and mental attitudes that can cause dysfunctions. They "short circuit" certain physiological processes of the body. Too much negative energy will weaken the muscles. If we test a chakra area and find it weak, there is a great likelihood that the physiological systems associated with that chakra are also weak. We can use color and other vibrational remedies to balance and strengthen it.

A muscle test gives us tangible feedback about our energies and their health. It is not foolproof, but it provides a starting point for greater self-awareness and responsibility.

And, it is simple. You do not need extensive knowledge about the body's muscular system to do it. You will need to know the general location of the chakra centers of the body. Here's how to conduct a muscle test for another person:

1. Choose a chakra center to be tested. If you wish, you can test them all, but for now it is only important to experience how the process works.

2. Have the individual to be tested extend one of his or her arms out to the side, with the opposite hand placed over the chakra point to be tested. Refer to the Determining Color Through a Muscle Test illustration on page 65.

3. Place your own hand upon the wrist of the person's outstretched arm. As you apply pressure downward, have the other person resist you. Do not force the arm down with your strength.

Rather, apply enough pressure to move the arm only a couple inches. Apply the pressure gradually and release it gradually. The muscle response will either be strong in the first part, locking into place, or it will give. Does the arm lock or does it feel mushy? With practice, you will be able to attune to the strength and resistance.

4. Having determined the present strength of the chakra, it is time to demonstrate how it can be short-circuited by our thoughts and emotions. This is an essential step in helping people overcome doubts they may have about the effectiveness of various holistic health practices. Using the guides from chapter 4, have the individual focus upon one of the emotional or mental attitudes that can create dysfunction within a chakra center.

5. When the emotion or mental attitude is in mind, retest the individual. You will find that the individual's muscle response will be noticeably weaker. This tangibly demonstrates that emotions and attitudes affect us on physiological levels. This is also why it is important to be aware of the range of emotions you are exposed to and experience throughout the day. If you don't rebalance those chakras affected by the emotions, physical disease is more likely to manifest.

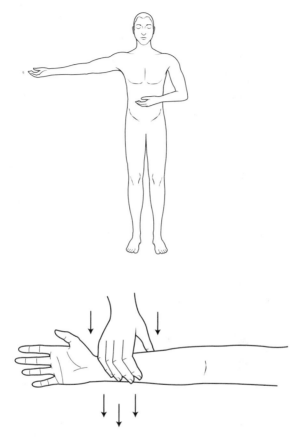

Determining Color Through a Muscle Test

Begin by having the individual extend one arm and place the hand of the other over a chakra point to be tested. This establishes a connection between the chakra and the muscle strength. With steady pressure upon the wrist of the extended arm, push down. The resistance provides tangible feedback.

6. Having demonstrated how the chakras and the corresponding physical responses can be short-circuited, it is important to demonstrate how vibration, in the form of color, can help. This is a good process to go through before applying any color therapy. It eliminates doubts and it makes the individual more receptive to the treatment.

7. Using any of the color healing methods in this book, apply color to the tested chakra for fifteen to thirty seconds. Now employ the muscle test once more. If you have correctly used the color healing method, there will be a noticeable improvement.

This muscle test can also be done on yourself. It can be used with any muscle of the body. The electrical system of the body and the chakras are tied intimately to the functions of all muscles in the body, voluntary and involuntary. The self-testing method should be done daily, as it does not take much time and it prevents imbalances from building up.

One of the easiest ways to self-test is to use your fingers. Mentally bring your mind to focus upon a particular chakra point of the body. You do not have to place your hands on it. Concentrate upon it. As you concentrate upon this chakra center, bring the index finger and thumb of one hand together tightly. With the index finger of your other hand, try and separate the circled thumb and finger. If the chakra is weak, the thumb and

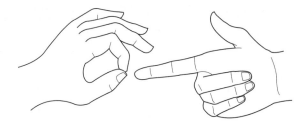

If the chakra you focus upon is strong and balanced, the response of whatever muscle you test will also be strong and balanced. It should be difficult to separate the thumb and index finger when testing a balanced chakra.

If the chakra being focused upon is weak, then the thumb and index finger are easily separated. Applying a beneficial color to that chakra will strengthen both the chakra and the muscle response.

A Muscle Test for Yourself

index finger will be easily separated. If it is strong, they will stay together.

For self-testing, it is beneficial to balance your entire chakra system first. Then, test your muscles by using your fingers. Learn to recognize when the energies are strong. Test your muscles periodically throughout the day. Is the resistance as strong as when you are balanced? The response of the muscles provides us with tangible feedback. They give us a starting point in determining our color needs and the area of application.

Applying the Color Once the Needs Are Identified

Sometimes, identifying the color can be the easiest part. It is the method of application, the length of application, and other factors that can be confusing. Throughout this book you are given a variety of color application techniques. In chapter 2 we discussed one that involves using your own hands and thoughts to send colored energy to another person (or to yourself). This will be elaborated upon, as will other techniques.

Once you have identified the color(s) needed, it is simply a matter of applying them in some fashion. This part requires you to find which method works most effectively for you. Any of the following methods are effective (all of them are described in this book):

- Apply color to a specific chakra to effect a change in its related physiological element.

- Project a color through your hands into the area of the body that is unbalanced.

- Perform color breathing to fill your body with the appropriate colored energy.

- Drink color-charged water.

- Lay colored cloth swatches upon the chakra or area of body that needs treatment.

- Use a slide projector for color therapy.

- Use colored candles to assist in the healing session.

Six
Color Therapy with Air and Water

Two of the most essential elements of life are air and water. We cannot survive very long without either one. Most people do not drink enough water or get enough fresh air. Simply increasing both is sure to boost our overall energy levels. We can also use both air and water in color therapy to assist the body in healing itself of various conditions.

Fresh air and proper breathing are essential to overall health and vitality. Breathing for the most beneficial effects should be done through the nostrils. Many people have the bad habit of mouth breathing, not realizing that nostril breathing is more natural and healthy. Mouth breathing makes an individual more susceptible to illness. It impairs the overall energy and it can weaken the constitution. Between the mouth and the lungs there is nothing to strain the air. Dust, dirt, and other impure substances have a clear track to the lungs. Mouth breathing also admits cold air to the lungs, which can lead to inflammation of the respiratory organs.

Nostril breathing, on the other hand, is healthier and more vitalizing to our entire energy system. The nostrils and the nasal passages have small hairs that are designed to filter and sieve the air. The nasal passages also warm the air through the mucous membranes. This makes the air more fit for the delicate organs of the lungs. Breath is then more energizing.

Focused deep breathing helps transform the air we breathe into energy. The vibrancy of that energy is affected by thought and method. With proper focus, you can breathe air into different parts of the body. Eventually this air can transform into different frequencies of energy.

One of the most beneficial breathing exercises is to use the early morning air to infuse the body with energy. Take a seated position outdoors. Place the tip of the tongue to the roof of the mouth, just behind the upper front teeth. Inhale through the nose for a slow count of five. Hold the breath for a count of five. Then, slowly exhale through the mouth for a count of five.

Have your eyes closed as you perform this exercise. Visualize air filling your entire body with invigorating energy that heals and strengthens. Remember that you are also breathing in light and all of the colors it contains. Perform this exercise for ten to fifteen minutes every morning. You will be amazed at how much more vibrant and energized you remain throughout the day.

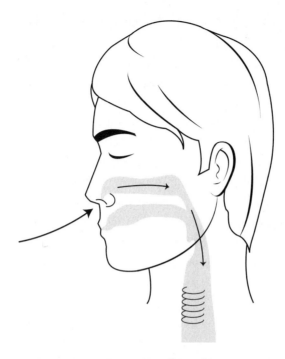

Proper Nostril Breathing

Breathing in through the nostrils is healthier. The nasal passages, with the help of the mucous membranes, filter the air and warm it. In order to have an idea energize your breath, you must inhale through the nose, with the tongue pressed against the roof of the mouth (just behind the upper front teeth). The exhalation is then through the mouth. This activates two major energy pathways, creating an invigorating energy orbit throughout the body.

You will become less fatigued and less aggravated by outside energies and intrusions. Performing this rhythmic breathing periodically throughout the day will also balance your system, relieve stress, and restore your overall vitality.

Proper breathing should involve the diaphragm. Place your hands gently upon your navel. Inhale deeply. Do your hands move outward? Exhale slowly. Do your hands move back in? If so, you are breathing properly from the diaphragm. If your hand movements are reversed, you breathe from the upper chest. In these cases, the air is not taken deeply into the body, and less energy and vitality are achieved from breathing.

Another generally beneficial breathing technique is to create an orbit of energy up the back of the body and down the front. In Taoist forms of healing it is often referred to as the "microcosmic orbit." We have various nerve pathways throughout the body. Two of these pathways are extremely important to our overall health and the proper functioning of our chakras. The first pathway is called the Governing Meridian. It begins at the perineum. This is a point located between the anal orifice and the sex organs. It extends up the spine and through the brain and back down to the roof of the mouth. The second pathway is called the Conception Meridian. It also begins at the perineum, but it runs up the front of the body and ends at the tip of the tongue.

Inhale = Diaphragm Expands   Exhale = Diaphragm Contracts

Inhale through the nose for a specified count. Hold the breath for the same count, and then exhale out the mouth, again, for the same count.

You should be able to feel the diaphragm expand with each breath.

Proper Rhythmic Breathing

The tongue is a trigger. When the tongue is placed against the roof of the mouth, behind the front teeth, it connects the two channels of energy. The air that we breathe is converted into energy, which can then be circulated up the spine and down the front of the body. This circulation is accomplished by focused thought and proper positioning of the tongue while breathing.

This orbit of energy circles up the spine and back down the front of the body. It energizes the major organs of the body and the entire nervous system, vitalizing and healing them. By working with breath, color, and the microcosmic orbit, we can more easily pump energy into different areas of the body. You will find, as you sit in meditation performing deep breathing, that the energy loop occurs naturally, and you will become more aware of it. You will begin to feel a warmth in the loop, as it strengthens the chakra activity of the body. Try this exercise:

Begin with rhythmic breathing. As you breathe, begin to feel the energy rising up the spine on the inhalation and down the front of the body on the exhalation. Since all energy follows thought, the energy from the air you are breathing will automatically circulate in the way that your thoughts direct it to circulate. Do not force it; you will feel it naturally beginning to flow in this pattern.

When the energy circulating in this orbit reaches the bottom-most point, visualize this orbit of energy turning and flowing through the body as the color red. Allow the red energy to circle several times, and then allow it all to

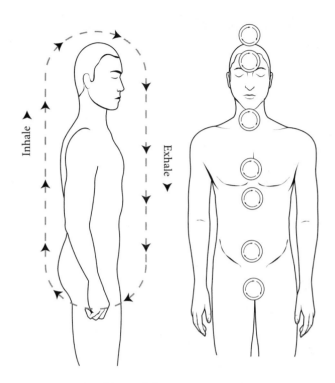

Inhale

Exhale

Breathing and the Microcosmic Orbit

Each circle of energy strengthens the chakra, causing stronger clockwise rotation and strengthening related physical energies. To create the microcosmic orbit, perform rhythmic breathing to increase your energy. As you continue to do that, feel the energy circulating up the spine and down the front of your body. As it circulates, feel it energizing your chakra centers. You may even wish to see each orbit change to a different color, one for each chakra.

gather in the base chakra, strengthening it. Visualize this center as a powerful vortex where energy spins in and out of the body in a clockwise direction. See it as a miniature dynamo.

Focus on the circuit of pure energy again. Now see it as a circuit of orange energy that circulates through the body along this orbital path. After several strong orbits, allow it all to gather in the spleen chakra. Continue this same process with all of the chakras and their colors.

After circulating the colors for each chakra, return to focusing and circulating pure energy along the microcosmic orbit. This exercise is extremely healing and energizing. It helps to prepare the individual to control and direct energy inside the body for various uses. It revitalizes body, mind, and spirit. It connects us with our most primal creative energy, helping us to release it more dynamically. It ultimately can be used to control the sexual energy for alchemical purposes.

General Color Breathing

There are simpler ways to do color breathing. Performing color breathing outdoors or by an open window can be very effective. Remember that air is turned into energy within the body. The frequency and strength of that energy is largely determined by our thoughts. Breathing different colors will assist with different health factors. The key is to determine which colors are needed. And we've already discussed guidelines for determining colors in previous chapters. Now would be a good time to try this exercise:

Make yourself comfortable. A seated position may be more comfortable. Your spine should be erect. Place the tip of the tongue against the roof of the mouth, just behind the front teeth. Inhale slowly through the nostrils for a count of five or six. Hold that breath for a slow count of twelve. Then, slowly exhale through the mouth for a count of five or six. Establish a slow rhythm.

Now, as you breathe in, see and feel the air coming in as a particular color. See and feel it filling your whole body. See and feel it balancing and healing whatever condition you are wanting to correct. If unsure as to the color, breathe in pure, crystalline white light. You may also simply breathe the seven colors of the rainbow to balance your overall system.

"Breathing the color" for three to five minutes can have a wonderful effect. Different colors, even when being "breathed," will elicit different effects.

Red Breath

Energizing and warming. Helps with colds and sinuses; drying to mucous membranes.

Pink Breath

Beneficial to skin conditions, especially puffiness. Eases loneliness.

Orange Breath

Balances emotions, eases respiratory conditions, awakens creativity, restores joy of life. Orange and pink combinations (peachy colors) are good for muscles.

Yellow Breath

Assists in learning easily. Eases indigestion and gas. The gold shade of yellow is an overall healing color and is beneficial for inner head problems.

Green Breath

Eases nervous conditions, awakens greater sense of prosperity, helps in overcoming bad habits. Pale green is good for improved vision.

Blue Breath

Calming, awakens artistic talents, eases respiratory problems. Generally healing for all children.

Dark Blue Breath

Accelerates healing and mending after surgery; helps heal bones when combined with a tinge of green (teal blue). Helps to open intuition.

Turquoise Breath

Helpful for respiratory conditions and arthritis. Combined with pink, it assists in overcoming bad eating habits.

Violet Breath

Beneficial to skeletal problems. Purifies, detoxifies the body, awakens spiritual attunement.

Purple Breath

Helpful in detoxifying the system. Helps overcome strong obsessions and negative feelings. Most effective when combined with white.

The techniques to control the breath and activate color energies can easily be adapted for use in healing sessions conducted for another person. We can transmit color healing by breathing upon the individual. Try this:

1. After determining the color most appropriate for the condition, have the individual recline.

2. Locate the troubled area. Gently lay a cloth swatch in the appropriate color over it.

3. As you gently hold the swatch in place, begin rhythmic breathing to increase your energy flow. See and feel yourself filling with that particular color vibration.

4. Lean forward, bringing your mouth close to the cloth swatch. As you exhale, breath heavily upon it. See and feel your colored breath (energy) penetrating the body and restoring balance. The warmth of the breath serves as a catalyst to activate the color vibrations. Continue this breathing

for several minutes or until you intuitively are
aware that the healing process has begun.

This color breathing method of healing is very effective
in easing and alleviating pain. It is quite effective for
headaches, cramps, and nerve pains. The same kind of
healing can also be effected by breathing color into the
chakra area.

Color Therapy with Water

Water is almost as essential to us as air. Most people do
not drink enough water. One of the most beneficial habits an individual can develop is to drink lots of water
every day. Drinking several tumblers upon arising in the
morning and before going to bed is a good practice. It
helps to flush out the system.

One of the most common complaints about drinking water comes from those who have trouble with water
retention. Unfortunately, these individuals do not understand what their body is doing. When our body does
not get enough water, it begins to retain it, shifting into a
kind of starvation mode. When we drink lots of water
during the day, the body does not feel as if it must retain
it; it is no longer "starved" for water.

We can magnetize or charge our water with various
color frequencies to assist us in healing and activating
various energies within the body. There are several ways

to charge water. The first way is to simply take a glass and fill it with water. Hold it in one hand, and hold your second hand over the glass about three to five inches from it. Begin rhythmic breathing, and focus upon a particular color. See and feel this color radiating out of your hand and into the water. Concentrate upon instilling the glass of water with the particular healing color vibration. Three to five minutes of concentration will magnetize the water strongly. You can then sip it or take it in various doses to help alleviate a condition.

You can also change water by using colored jars. Fill the colored jars with water, and set them out in the early morning sun. The sun will activate the color of the jar and infuse the water with its particular vibration. You can drink this to help ease the particular problem.

Yet another method of infusing water with a particular color vibration is to wrap a jar or bottle in a colored cloth or colored paper. Set the jar in the early morning sun. As the sun hits the colored wrap, it activates the color frequency and instills the water with it. One to three hours in the morning light is an effective length of time. You can charge several jars of water at one time and store them, making enough to drink for several days.

Taking a piece of colored cardboard and setting it on top of a glass or jar of water will also infuse the water with the color frequency. It is the sunlight that serves as an activating and transmitting force in this color healing method.

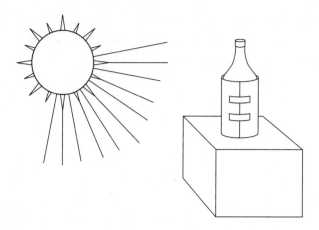

Wrap a jar or bottle in a colored cloth, paper, etc. Set the jar in the morning sun. The sunlight activates the color and transmits it into the water. Drinking such charged water is a form of color therapy.

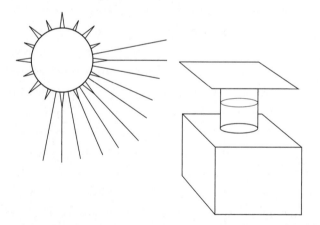

Setting colored cardboard upon a glass or jar of water will similarly charge it with a particular color vibration. Even a colored stone or crystal can be used to energize the water for color therapy.

Healing with Colored Water

For those who enjoy using crystals and stones, putting different colored stones and gems into the water will also charge it with a particular color frequency. You must be careful with this, as most crystals and gems have a unique electromagnetic frequency, as well as a color energy. This can change how the water affects you, possibly increasing the "charge." A study of various crystals and stones will help you to discern what other kinds of effects the stones could have upon the water, other than its color frequency.

Seven
Projecting Colors

There is a variety of ways to project colors for therapeutic purposes. Most of these are easily learned and developed by the average individual. We can all learn to apply color therapy to assist in maintaining and restoring our own health and vibrancy. Color therapy is not a substitute for other forms of medicine and therapy, but it is something that enables us to become more active and responsible in our own healing process.

We have already learned that we are more than just physical substance. We are composed of other, more subtle energy fields. We have also seen that there are ways of interacting with these subtle energies to create changes in physical conditions. For those who are interested in pursuing holistic healing, incorporating color therapy into their own practices, or seeing color as a means of helping themselves on physical and subtle levels, the methods in this chapter will be of great benefit.

The Touch of Color

Earlier, we demonstrated how we can radiate energy outward from our hands by breathing and by concentrating our thoughts. This first form of healing with color has always been considered more of a "spiritual" form. Unfortunately, when you mention that you do spiritual healing, many individuals assume that it is healing based solely upon faith and the healer's alignment with some divine force.

Although the healing touch can be enhanced by faith, its effectiveness is not dependent upon faith or the divine. (Unless one recognizes that the divine operates in each one of us and thus can be accessed by each of us.) How the healing process actually takes place is still poorly understood. Even so, it is important to acknowledge that when we perform certain acts, there will be certain effects. We all have the capability to create changes within our physical and subtle energies—even if we don't understand it all. It is innate. What we must do is learn the techniques that enable us to awaken and channel this energy for various purposes.

Keep in mind that healing always comes from within. It is the patient who heals him- or herself. You may be a catalyst, and an assistant to boost the individual's own recuperative system, but the healing must come from within.

Before you begin a healing session for another person, know what you are going to do. Understand the process. Understand which colors you need to use for the condition. Try and understand the metaphysical causes of the physical dis-ease, and discuss this with the individual. Make no claims. Explain how our energy system operates. Perform some muscle testing to prove it, if necessary, and simply present yourself as someone who would like to help.

Never work on another person if you are tired or ill. Although it's true that when we work to heal another we in turn are healed, working on another while we demonstrate illness can set up mental blocks and hinder the receptivity of the healing colors and energy.

Healing Through Touch

You are becoming a channel of color energy. As you breathe, you pull energy down through you and radiate it out your hands to heal and balance others. The energy takes on the frequency of your thoughts and focus. As you concentrate on a particular color, the radiations take that frequency, and the color is absorbed by the person being treated. The process heals and balances, and it awakens your higher intuition and sensitivities. Here is an exercise to further your skills as a healer:

1. Center yourself before you begin. Relax. Perform some rhythmic breathing.

2. Have the individual being treated recline in front of you. Extend your hands over the individual about three to six inches.

3. Visualize pure crystalline energy pouring down through the top of your head, filling your body. Eventually this energy overflows; see and feel it pouring down your arms and out your hands.

4. Begin with white, crystalline energy. Holding your hands over the crown of the individual's head, see and feel this white light pouring through you and into the other person. See his or her whole body and energy field becoming charged, strengthened, and balanced. Continue this for several minutes. Stop when you feel comfortable with it. Working with healing helps you attune to your higher self. Listen to it.

5. Now move to the particular problem area. Continue your rhythmic breathing. Focus your mind on the color needed for the problem. See the energy pouring out through you to that area, balancing and healing it. See it becoming stronger as the color radiations are absorbed. Visualize the energy cleansing, balancing, and healing the immediate imbalanced area, as well as the entire system with which it is associated.

6. Next, move to the chakra(s) closest to the problem area. For example, if there is a stomach upset, begin by working on that particular area of the body. First see the entire digestive system being balanced and healed. Move your hands

and attention to the solar plexus chakra, which mediates the energies of the digestive system and the stomach. Project balancing energy to the chakra by using its appropriate color.

7. Move on to the base chakra area. Radiate red energy to energize and strengthen it. Do this for several minutes. Then, move up to each of the seven chakras, projecting the appropriate colors. This balances the entire chakra system, and it strengthens the overall healing process.

8. To conclude the healing, you may return to the head area and project white, crystalline energy through you into the individual. See and feel it pouring into your head and out of your hands, filling the individual's entire being with strength and vibrancy.

Light Projections in Healing

There are a number of ways in which we can use colored lights for therapeutic purposes. The simplest is by sitting under the light generated by colored light bulbs. As you sit under the lights, breathe deeply and regularly, knowing your body will absorb the energy. The variety of colors available in light bulbs is somewhat limited, but there is another way of projecting colored light. We can make our own slides. Using a normal slide projector, we can simply and quickly project lights in various combinations. Slide projectors are rather inexpensive, and many can be found in discount stores and pawn shops for next to nothing. The next step is to make your own slides.

Most camera stores have inexpensive blank slide frames for sale. Filter paper of various colors can be cut to fit inside the frame. The colored filter paper (or "light gels") can be purchased at a theatrical supply store. If you do not have access to a theatrical store, many school and office supply stores carry plastic sheets for overhead projectors. These also come in a variety of colors. If nothing else, the clear plastic sheets can be colored with overhead projector pens.

Making the slides is a simple task. Take your empty slide frame and open it up. Cut a square in your filter paper, so that it will cover the opening of the slide when the slide frame is closed. There should be enough space left around the color filter so that the two sides of the frame can be glued together. Place drops of glue around the edges of one side of the open frame. Hold the filter in place and close the slide frame over it. Press the two sides together until the glue sticks.

If you wish, you can make several sets of colored slides. It's good to have a basic set for energizing and strengthening chakras. This set should have the seven colors of the rainbow: red, orange, yellow, green, blue, indigo, and violet.

You can also add the inbetween shades and other colors that may be needed for general healing. A set like this allows you to fine-tune your healing techniques. Here are some of the colors this set may include:

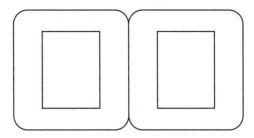

Open the slide frame. Cut the filter paper so that it covers the opening in the frame. Leave enough frame space around the filter so that the two sides of the frame can be glued together.

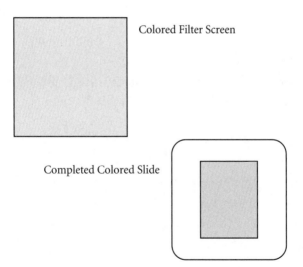

Colored Filter Screen

Completed Colored Slide

Set the filter over the opening, place glue around the outside edges of the frame, and then press together.

Making Colored Slides

Red	Red-orange	Orange
Yellow-orange	Yellow	Yellow-green
Green	Blue-green	Blue
Indigo	Blue-violet	Violet
Red-violet	Lemon	Turquoise
Purple	Magenta	Scarlet

You probably won't find all of these colors available in filter paper. You can still create them by including different filter papers in the same slide. The light of the projector will blend and activate the colors. The filter paper is thin, so several colors can be combined within the slide frame effectively. Refer back to the section on color combinations, if needed (pages 12–13). Otherwise, use the list below.

Creating Colors Through Combinations

Scarlet:	2 red filters
Red-orange:	2 red filters and 1 yellow filter
Orange:	1 red filter and 1 yellow filter
Yellow-orange:	2 yellow filters and 1 red filter
Yellow-green:	2 yellow filters and 1 blue filter
Green:	1 yellow filter and 1 blue filter
Blue-green:	3 blue filters and 1 yellow filter
Turquoise:	2 blue filters and 1 yellow filter
Indigo:	2 blue filters and 1 red filter

Violet:	1 red filter and 1 blue filter
Blue-violet:	2 blue filters and 1 red filter
Red-violet:	2 red filters and 1 blue filter
Magenta:	3 red filters and 1 blue filter
Purple:	1 yellow filter, 1 red filter, and 1 blue filter

Conducting a Light Healing Session

To conduct a light healing session with colored slides, first prepare the healing area: put the slides into the projector and set the projector opposite the area where the person to be healed will be sitting.

1. Have the individual take a seated position. Explain color breathing to the individual.

2. Ask the person to engage in color breathing as each colored slide is projected upon him or her. Have the person picture the projected light filling, energizing, and healing the particular condition. For a rainbow effect, have the person visualize the colors entering through the crown chakra and filling the entire body.

3. Go through the necessary colors, leaving each color on the individual for two to three minutes. For chronic conditions, you may wish to do longer treatments. Again, don't be afraid to trust your own intuition in this process.

4. Close the session.

Note: The session can be ended beneficially in several ways. Using the green light at the end is effective. It balances the energy system of the individual. However, you do not want to use this in conditions that are cancerous or tumorous, as green helps things to grow. You may wish to simply run the color for each chakra, starting with the base and moving to the crown. If you are concerned about the green, substitute a pink or white light for the heart center.

You can also use this technique to heal and balance yourself. You may even wish to use the slides to assist in meditation. Remember, the colors affect more than just the physiological systems of the body. They also activate our subtle energies and levels of consciousness. If, for example, you have difficulty relaxing in your meditation, sit under the blue light while meditating. Experiment. Have fun. Color projections are powerful and effective.

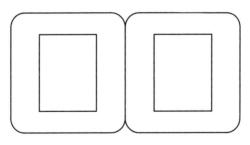

Using Colored Slides to Heal

Long-Distance Color Healing

Absentee or long-distance healing can be an effective tool to assist those who cannot be present for a healing session. This is similar to the concept of people sending prayers and healing to others. We can enhance this technique through the various color techniques discussed within this book.

The phenomenon of long-distance healing is nothing new. It does transcend logical thought processes, but it in no way transcends reality. Energy operates on all levels and is in many ways not yet understood. That which is referred to as psychic energy is the creative life force of all substance. It surrounds us, penetrates us, and is a part of us. It can be controlled and directed, molded and shaped, stored and used. It can be controlled by the mind.

We know that the human body is a biochemical, electromagnetic energy system, but our psychic energy is the basic building block. The biochemical and electromagnetic aspects are the physical expressions of our psychic life force. This psychic life force operates on a level that transcends physical time and space.

Quantum physics has done much to explain the phenomenon of psychic energy. It teaches us that all life and all energy expressions are connected. Because we are energy, operating on many levels and in many forms, we cannot move without influencing everything in our universe. Every time we observe something, we are changed, and so is what we are observing. With higher expressions and focuses of energy, time, and space are transcended. Thus, in long-distance healing we experience the individual as if he or she were in immediate proximity, regardless of actual time and location.

Colors can be used to assist us in concentrating, tuning, and transmitting healing energies. They also assist us in achieving a transcendent level of consciousness, allowing us to employ a more concentrated focus of our psychic energy. We are then developing a controlled use of mind through the power of color.

For long-distance healing, it is beneficial to have a "witness." A witness is a term that has come to be used in the field of radionics. It is "anything which will psychically represent the subject."[1] A witness can be a photo,[2] signature, blood specimen, hair clipping, nail clipping, or anything that can provide a link between you and the person to whom you wish to direct the colors. The witness helps us to link the rational and the intuitive levels of the mind, thus serving to awaken the process of sending energy at a distance.

The witness assists us in creating a thoughtform and in directing it toward the individual more effectively. Through the witness, you are more easily able to estab-

---

1. Charles W. Cosimano, *Psionics 101*, p. 82.

2. A Polaroid photograph is considered most effective by many people, in that it will capture the entire positive and negative ion field around the individual, while a photo developed from a negative will only capture half of the field; thus, it is not considered as strong of a link.

lish resonance. It serves to awaken the connection beyond physical levels. It brings the individual "to mind."
The healing energy can then be sent regardless of time
and space.

Take time before sending the healing energy to determine which color(s) will be most beneficial. If unsure,
send white light. You may wish to use your pendulum to
determine the colors needed. Hold your left hand over the
picture (or witness); and with the right hand using the
pendulum, ask questions concerning the colors needed by
the individual.

Once the healing colors are discerned, you must then
proceed to project the healing energies. There are several
effective ways to do this.

1. You may simply do it through your ability to visualize. Hold the witness between your two
   hands. If you do not have a witness, hold the individual's image within your mind. Begin rhythmic breathing. As you focus on the individual,
   see and feel the energy radiating through you
   and out to him or her. Visualize this color surrounding the person and permeating his or her
   system. Visualize the condition being balanced
   and healed. Perform this for about ten minutes.

2. You may wish to use the slide projector. Tape the
   picture (or witness) to a white piece of poster
   board. Shine the colors of the seven chakras upon
   it for about thirty seconds each. Then focus the

primary healing color on the picture for ten to fifteen minutes.

You can confidently go about your business, knowing the color radiations will seek out the individual. This is very effective to do at night, when you know the individual is likely to be asleep. There are less distractions, and the effects of the colors are more easily absorbed.

3. You may also wish to use the color radiations from candles to assist you in projecting long-distance healing energies. (Use the following chapter as a guideline.) Simply place the witness next to a particular candle or in one of the candle healing patterns described in the next chapter. Do this for fifteen to thirty minutes per day.

When conducting any healing, it is always good to affirm: "for the good of all, according to the free will of all." In this manner, the healing occurs in the most beneficial way for the individual's growth. We do not have the right to intrude upon the free will of others. Since this technique is a dynamic way of affecting people in subtle (often unnoticed) yet very real ways, we must be cautious.

Opinions differ as to whether or not one should project healing toward others without their permission. I am of the school of taking great personal responsibility for one's life and actions, and the only one who knows what is ultimately best for an individual is that individual.

Everyone has the right to make mistakes. It is often through our mistakes that our greatest growth can occur. If we interfere, we may rob the individual of a learning experience critical to his or her evolution. Besides, it takes hardly any energy to ask someone if you can help.

These are not hard and fast rules. Obviously, if there is someone under your care such as children, you act in accordance with what you, as an adult, know best. There are always exceptions, but you must make your decisions, especially your healing ones, with a willingness to take full responsibility for the consequences of your actions—positive or negative. If you cannot do this, then you do not need to be dabbling in the healing energies.

Keep in mind that you are not practicing medicine—there are many laws against diagnosing and prescribing. We cannot prescribe colors like we can medication. When we use the tools of vibrational healing we are employing preventive care, along with holistic maintenance. Taking money for using color on someone must be approached cautiously, as the laws are very strict about practicing medicine without a license. I personally do not charge for my healing sessions, nor do I take donations. I do make a suggestion that the individual either donate to a charity or pass a favor on anonymously to someone else. I do know a number of licensed massage therapists who employ color in their work, but it is used as a tool within the massage process, and as they are licensed, there is no problem.

Do not be afraid to experiment. The extent of the healing effects of color is still not completely determined or understood. Find what works for you.

Eight

Healing with Candles

Fire has always been regarded as something holy. In many ancient cultures, the manner in which smoke melted into the air was magical. The origin of fire was just as magical and mysterious. In most societies, fire first belonged to the gods, and the tales and myths of the great fire-stealers still live today within our books and lore. Prometheus and the creation of humanity is but one example. (Prometheus stole fire from the gods to give it to humanity.)

Fire operates in all of our lives, in physical and subtle ways. The fires from the sun sustain life upon the earth. The fires of passion bring inspiration and creativity. Fire operates in all aspects of life. From volcanic fires to the fires of ordinary body heat, from the solar fires to the fires of intellect, fire's presence is felt nearly everywhere.

Candles have been used for metaphysical purposes for about as long as fire has been around. The candle is a very powerful symbol for the activation of more fire and light in our lives, on physical and subtle levels. When we use the fires of candles, we are participating in the ritual of fire that has existed throughout the ages, from the lighting of the stars to the lighting of hearthstones of companionship and community.

The practice of using candles for healing should be seen as an ancient rite of creation. When you light the candle, imagine you are creating light where there was no light before, bringing warmth and healing where it is needed. This imaging in itself is extremely healing. See the unlit candle as the unlit essence of life energy in the physical body that awaits a renewing touch of fire to help restore health to body and soul.

Fundamental Rules for Candle Use

1. The color of the candle and its vibrational force are activated, released, and amplified when the candle is lit. As it burns, the color is released into the surrounding area and affects those within that area.

2. The color of the candle is determined by the kind of healing needed. Consult the list of correspondences on page 22.

3. All candles should be cleansed and blessed before their use. This serves to cleanse the candle of any negativity it may have accumulated and

absorbed during its making. It strengthens the color so that it works far more effectively for your purpose. This process is called "dressing the candle."

This dressing of the candle is done with an oil. There are several candle-anointing oils on the market. You can also use a simple olive oil. Always rub the candle in the same direction. For healing candles, it is beneficial to rub them from bottom to top. This is symbolic of bringing the color out of the candle and into the atmosphere.

Do not worry if you do not have an oil to use. Simply using a strong affirmation that relates to your purpose or reciting a favorite prayer as you dress the candle are effective methods. It prepares the candle, and it prepares you.

4. Once you have used a candle for a specific purpose, it should not be used for something else. This will set up conflicting vibrations.

5. Any candle will be effective. For longer, more sustained effects, church candles can be quite effective. They come encased in glass containers and they can burn for a week at a time.

6. Do not use candles to interfere with the free will of another. The rebound effect is never very pleasant.

7. Extinguishing the candle should be the last act in the healing process. It should be performed

with strong intention, as if you are firmly setting and locking the healing energy in place. It
is preferable that breath not be used to extinguish the candle. Breath, like fire, is creative, and
a creative force should not be used to extinguish
another creative force. Use a small cup or a tin-
foil cone to extinguish the flame.

Candle Colors

Candles have tremendous thoughtforms associated with
them. The colors of the candles will elicit therapeutic effects in the same manner as colored cloth or colored light.
Candles have been used not only for healing but also for
prayer, meditation, and magical purposes. It is a good
idea to understand these metaphysical associations with
candles before you use them.

White

The white candle is a symbol of purity and power. It amplifies the effects of any other burning candle. It pro-
motes cleansing and awakens hope. It can be used to
initiate new energy movement in healing or in other av-
enues. Unless it is an extremely cheap candle, when a
white candle smokes, it indicates that the negativity in
the area is being burnt off. When the smoking ceases, the
area is cleansed.

Black

The black candle is very powerful. It is also one of the most protective. It can be used to bring a person back down to earth. It can also be used in various rituals to uncover secrets and for understanding the purpose of sacrifices we have made. It can be used in meditation to help us find the light within the dark. It is stabilizing and awakens greater responsibility. It is most effective when burnt with a white candle. Too much black can manifest depression.

Red

The red candle is a symbol of love and health and the attainment of ambitions. It is the color and candle of passion and sexual potency, which are expressions of our primal life force.

Pink

The pink candle is a symbol of love and success. It awakens a consciousness of clean living and honor. It stimulates purity of intention, and it can awaken a vision of truth and success.

Orange

The orange candle is a symbol of joy and creativity. It can be used with meditations to stimulate spiritual attainment. It can help to attract people, animals, and other things you want in your life.

Yellow and Gold

Yellow is the color of the candle's flame. It is associated with meditation. In it we can learn to see the fulfillment of our desires. The gold shades assist in understanding and stimulating dream activity.

Green

This is the candle of growth and movement. It balances the energies of the body and mind. It can help open levels of consciousness that are aware of the nature spirits in our life. It can stimulate greater youthfulness, abundance, and fertility.

Blue

The blue candle is a symbol of spiritual understanding. It awakens our innate abilities to perceive. It is also a symbol of life, and it awakens within the consciousness a greater faith in life's processes. It is powerfully healing for children. Blue candles have been known to be burned in various rituals to bring in quick money.

Gray and Silver

This candle color is a symbol of clarity. You can meditate upon it to see how best to initiate new activities. It awakens that level of the subconscious mind that is aware of how the wheels of life are turning for you. It is a good candle to burn when studying astrology, as it assists in gaining a new understanding of the stellar influences. It awakens our most innate primal intuition.

Brown

Brown is a neutral candle. It is grounding. It can awaken greater discernment and certainty. It can also be meditated upon to help uncover lost articles. It is a color associated with St. Anthony, who is the patron saint of lost things.

Violet and Purple

These are symbols of spirituality, power, and mastery. They awaken success, elevation, and attainment of spiritual desires.

Healing Methods with Candles

When we light a candle, the color energy is released into the atmosphere. There it can be absorbed by the individual. Simply being in the area of the candle is enough to allow you to be affected. The energy released from the candle will be absorbed through your auric field and taken into the body itself. The more focused you are on that process, the quicker and more effective it is. Breathing in the energy will also amplify the effects.

One of the most beneficial and powerful means of using candles in healing is by arranging them in geometric layouts around the individual being healed. The geometry of energy also has dynamic effects. Its interactions with the electromagnetic fields of humans serves as the basis of mandalas and talismans.

Different geometric shapes will alter and enhance the effects of colors. It simply involves understanding what the geometric layout will do, and then using that layout to arrange the candles around the individual to be healed. Here we will look at six basic layouts for candle therapy. They are all very powerful.

The Triangle

The triangle is an amplifier. It increases the power of the healing force of whatever color candle is being used. It also makes the color more cleansing.

The Square

Setting candles in the formation of a square around the individual stabilizes the entire physiological system. It calms and settles. It grounds and focuses the basic life force of the color being used.

The Cross

Placing candles in the form of a cross around the individual will help balance the four elements (fire, air, water, and earth) in the individual so that the color can work effectively. It affects the heart center and can be used for all problems associated with it. It balances our physical energies with our emotional, mental, and spiritual energies. It also stabilizes the electromagnetics of the body, providing assistance so that the color is more easily absorbed.

The Pentagram

The pentagram grounds and strengthens the color(s) being used. It awakens the individual's spiritual energies and calls upon those energies to assist with the healing process. The pentagram is also known to draw many of the healing angels, especially those known as the Cherubim.

The Six-Rayed Star

This candle layout is effective in helping to link the heart with mind, body, and spirit so that the healing can occur on all levels, not just the physical. It helps draw out the individual's own divine aspects to assist more fully in the healing process and the absorption of the color. It is strengthening and protective.

The Seven-Rayed Star

This is one of the most healing of candle layouts, especially for children. It balances and aligns all of the chakras so that the healing color can work most effectively. It is soothing to emotional and mental attitudes that may have precipitated the physical illness. It amplifies the healing energies of the colors.

The triangle amplifies.

The square stabilizes.

The cross balances and aligns.

Healing Layouts with Candles

The pentagram strengthens.

The six-rayed star links the mind
and the heart for overall healing.

The seven-rayed star is the most
healing of layouts.

Healing Layouts with Candles

The first task in healing with candles, as in any form of color healing, is to determine which color is needed. It may even be several colors. When we use candle layouts, we do not have to use just one color. We can use several colors simultaneously. We can either place a different colored candle in separate positions in the layout or set the various colors side by side at each position in the layout. Experiment and find what works best for you. You can use the following techniques for self-healing and to treat another person.

1. Having decided on the layout and the color(s), have the individual sit or recline in the middle of the layout.

2. Light the candles with intention. See the lighting of the candles as a creative act that is going to bring light, color, and energy to the condition.

3. As the individual sits within the layout, begin rhythmic breathing. As you inhale, visualize yourself drawing the color into your body and balancing the condition. Stay relaxed and breathe slowly. Allow the fire-charged color to work smoothly and naturally. Know that as your system is being healed and strengthened through this process, so is the system of the individual you're assisting.

4. Fifteen to twenty minutes is powerfully effective. If you find the time, and especially if you are working on self-healing, you may wish to do

this first thing in the morning and the last thing before you go to bed. The effects are cumulative. They stabilize, build, and support your entire energy system.

5. Do this daily until the condition is relieved. Continue a day or two after just to provide extra strength to that area.

Some individuals will continue the treatments daily until the candles have burnt themselves out. Again, experiment. There may be times when you feel better doing it that way, but there may also be times when all you need is one or two treatments. Trust your intuition and your body's response.

Absent Healing with Candles

We can also use candles and layouts to do long-distance healing. Again, it is good to have a witness (a photo or something the person has touched) to assist in the process. If you do not have a witness, write the individual's name and address on a piece of paper. Then, take a plain white taper candle, dress it (anointing it with oil to cleanse and bless it), and visualize it as a symbol of the spiritual and physical essence of the one to whom you are going to send healing energies.

If you are working with a witness, place the white candle on top of the item, taking care not to drip wax on it. If you are using paper (with the individual's name and address) or a photo, you may wish to use a candle holder to prevent wax from dripping on the item.

Arrange the candles according to the layout you have chosen, placing the white taper candle in the middle. Light the white candle, visualizing the energies of the person it represents becoming vibrant and full of life.

Light the colored candles. See and visualize the person being filled with healing energy. You may leave the candles burning for ten to fifteen minutes, or you may wish to stay and add your visualizations to the candle projections. You may even wish to place yourself in the layout, holding the witness and projecting colors from within the healing layout. Again, experiment. You will find that different methods of healing are necessary for different people.

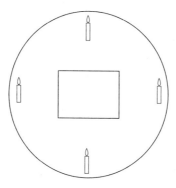

Absent Healing with Candles

Place the witness in the middle of the layout and arrange the colored candles accordingly. The color vibrations are then projected and aligned through the witness to the individual. You may wish to use a white taper candle to represent the witness. Simply light it and set it on top of the witness item. This strengthens the process.

Nine

The Tree of Colors

So far we have discussed some of the more traditional ways to understand and practice color healing. These were from a theosophical perspective, though they have been adapted into most major systems of metaphysics. However, it is by no means the only system for healing with colors.

No one system is any better or more effective than another. What is important is that you find a system that works for you. The more significance you can personally attach to it, the more receptive you will be to experiencing the healing influence of the color vibrations.

Different traditions have their own color correspondences. For example, astrological traditions assign specific colors to the various planets and signs of the zodiac. Since the signs and planets rule different parts of the body, the astrological colors can be used to heal specific areas. We can still employ the same healing techniques described earlier.

The Astrological Tradition of Colors: I

Planets	Parts of Body Ruled	Colors
Sun	Vitality, circulatory system, heart	Orange, Gold
Moon	Breasts, stomach, ovaries, body rhythms	Silver, Green
Mercury	Nervous system, hands, lungs, respiratory system	Metallic Blue
Venus	Physical appearance (hair, skin, etc.) reproductive system	Pastel Blue, Green
Mars	Red corpuscles, muscles, male genitals	Scarlet, Magenta
Jupiter	Liver, hips, thighs, cell nutrition	Deep Blue-Purple, Indigo
Saturn	Skin, bones, teeth, joints, ears (hearing)	Black, Dark Brown, Green
Uranus	Cones and rods in the eyes	Electric Blue, Silver
Neptune	Pineal gland, chakras	Sea Green, Smokey Gray
Pluto	Regenerative forces of the reproductive system	Magenta

The Astrological Tradition of Colors: II

Signs of Zodiac	Parts of Body Ruled	Colors
Aries	Head, face, brain	Red
Taurus	Neck, throat, thyroid	Light Blue, Pastel
Gemini	Hands, shoulders, arms, lungs	Slate Blue, Lemon Yellow
Cancer	Stomach, breasts	Silver, Green
Leo	Heart, back	Orange, Gold
Virgo	Intestines, bowels	Deep Blue
Libra	Kidneys, ovaries	Soft Pink, Blue
Scorpio	Sex organs, bladder, nose	Deep Yellow, Bright Red
Sagittarius	Hips, thighs, muscles	Deep Blue
Capricorn	Knees, joints, skin	Black, Brown, Dark Green
Aquarius	Calves, ankles, eyes	Electric Blue, Pale Yellow, Green
Pisces	Feet, toes, lymph glands	Sea Green, Silver

(The signs and planets can indicate a greater propensity for problems in their corresponding body parts, especially if they are found in the sixth house of the astrological chart. The sixth house is the house of health, work, and service.)

One of the most effective alternative color-healing systems is that of the mystical Qabala. The Qabala is an ancient form of mysticism with many philosophical and pragmatic dimensions. On one level, it teaches how the universe was formed through ten stages. On a more practical level, it teaches how to access different levels of our consciousness so that we can tap our personal energies and the energies of the universe more effectively.

The Tree of Life is the primary symbol and image for working with the Qabala system. It is a diagram with ten levels. Each represents a specific level of the subconscious mind. Each of these levels is connected to different physiological processes, as well as creative and metaphysical processes. Over time, each of these levels has come to be associated with many different attributes, including specific colors. These correspondences, when utilized properly, activate a level within our subconscious mind. This triggers certain kinds of responses on physical and spiritual levels.

This book does not intend to explore all of these correspondences and their effects. For further information, you may wish to consult my earlier books on the Qabala (*Simplified Qabala Magic* and *Imagick*). In this chapter, we will concern ourselves only with how to use the Tree of Life in color healing. It is an alternate system, but it is powerfully effective.

A tree is an ancient symbol, and it is easily adapted as a metaphor for the human condition of health. The tree represents things that grow and evolve. It is the bridge between the heavens and the earth; like the roots and trunk of the tree, humans have their health foundation in the physical body. Still, we must pay attention to our more subtle expressions of energy as well. We cannot just focus on the physical body (the roots of our tree). For example, trees must be pruned to bear fruit. They need good soil, clean air, and water. The trunk and the upper branches are just as important to the health of the tree as the roots. A tree is liable to disease from insects, pollutants, and other outside sources. They will eventually work their way down from the upper branches into the root system. All of this affects the tree's ability to bear fruit.

The same is true of humans. If we don't keep our spiritual, mental, and emotional energies balanced, they will eventually work themselves down into our physical bodies, manifesting disease. We must learn to work with our energies on all levels. This is why in the next chapter we will explore healing with the four levels of colors in the Tree of Life. There is a color to help ease every problem— whether it's spiritual, mental, emotional, or physical.

Different levels of the subconscious mind control and mediate different energies of the body. The difficulty is in determining which level controls which bodily functions, and then determining how to activate that level of the subconscious more consciously. This is where the Qabalistic Tree of Life comes into play.

As I mentioned earlier, there are ten levels in the Tree of Life. You'll see in the illustration, on the opposite page, the traditional Hebrew title for each level has been given, along with its translation. Each is a symbol of a level within the subconscious mind.

The more we learn to consciously activate and access these levels, the more we can consciously control our health from all perspectives and all dimensions. Learning to consciously open up these levels of the subconscious will help trigger specific healing effects. It will not only directly influence various body functions, but it will also help us awaken to an understanding of the metaphysical stimuli behind the problem. We begin by learning something about the energies of each of these levels of the subconscious mind.

Malkuth

Basic Colors: Black, olive-green, russet, and citrine.

Astrological Influence: The earth.

Healing Archangel: Sandalphon (San-Dahl-Fon).

Body Functions Influenced: Overall physical health and
metabolism, feet, eliminative system. The body's first
line of defense against toxicity.

Malkuth is that level of the subconscious mind that oversees how our health is affected by our physical environment. It influences our overall physical health and stamina. Not all disease comes from mental or emotional causes. Pollution and other toxic environmental factors can serve as a catalyst to specific problems.

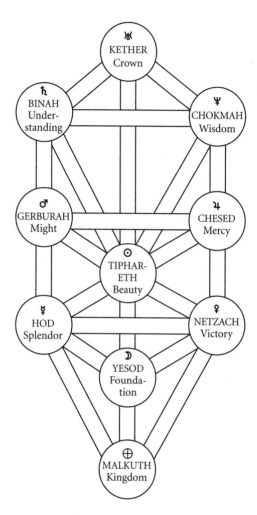

The Qabalistic Tree of Life

Each level controls and directs certain physiological processes of the body, and each also mediates other, more universal energies as well. These more universal energies include the play of astrological forces in our lives, contact with other dimensions (including members of the angelic hierarchy), and various creative and intuitive functions of the mind.

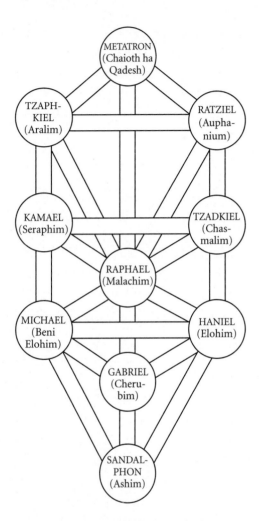

Healing Angels of the Tree of Life

It is through our feet that we are connected to the earth and all of its energy patterns, toxic or healing. Because we cannot control all environmental factors, it is good to regularly activate this level of the subconscious mind through color healing. It stabilizes most major systems.

Yesod

Basic Colors: Purple and violet.

Astrological Influence: The moon.

Healing Archangel: Gabriel (Gah-Bree-Ehl).

Body Functions Influenced: Sexual organs, breasts, stomach, lower extremities, digestive system. Pregnancy, body rhythms, lymphatics, menstruation and body secretions.

Yesod is that level of the subconscious that oversees sexual energy and development. It has ties to the Eastern concept of the kundalini: the primal, sacred life force. This is also the level of the subconscious that directs our body rhythms—the highs, the lows, the fluctuations we encounter on a daily and monthly cycle.

It is at this level of the subconscious that we can come to an understanding of how our emotions affect our overall health foundations. This is a level of the subconscious that can help us attune more psychically to our health or the health of another.

Hod

Basic Color: Orange.

Astrological Influence: Mercury.

Healing Archangel: Michael (Mee-Kah-Ehl).

Body Functions Influenced: Nervous system, respiratory system, lungs, hands, right hip, vocal cords (speech), memory, hearing and sight, pancreas.

Hod is that level of the subconscious mind that mediates the nervous and respiratory systems to a great degree. It has connections to the left hemisphere brain activities as well. Any kind of nervous, respiratory, or even intestinal problem can be alleviated by stimulating this level of the subconscious. It can also influence sugar-related diseases.

This is a level of the subconscious that we need to activate if we are having difficulty with communication in any form. It is a level that can facilitate receptiveness to all forms of doctoring. Specifically, it helps us learn more about the functioning of our own body—its strengths and weaknesses.

Netzach

Basic Color: Emerald.

Astrological Influence: Venus.

Healing Archangel: Haniel (Hah-Ni-Ehl).

Body Functions Influenced: All major aspects of physical appearance (skin, hair, etc.), female sex organs, reproduction, mammary glands, menstruation, throat, kidneys, the left hip area of the body, acid-alkaline balance, thyroid.

Netzach is that area of the subconscious mind that directs not only our physical appearance, but how we truly feel about it. It has ties to the kidneys and, to some degree, the eliminative system of the body. It influences the sex organs, especially in women, and it is a level that can be activated to ease menstrual problems, pregnancy difficulties, and any generative troubles.

Netzach is a level of the mind that is also connected to our emotional states. It can be useful to activate when physical problems are being complicated and intensified by emotional states. This level can be activated to facilitate healing through art therapy, color healings, and dance and movement therapies.

Tiphareth

Basic Color: Yellow (gold).

Astrological Influence: The sun.

Healing Archangel: Raphael (Rah-Fah-Ehl).

Body Functions Influenced: Overall vitality, functions of the heart, the circulatory system, the immune system, the thymus gland, metabolism, spinal cord, physical growth.

Tiphareth is a powerful level of the subconscious mind, especially in the healing process. If unsure as to which level of the subconscious you need to stimulate for healing a condition, you cannot go wrong by stimulating this one. It affects the entire body's metabolism and balance.

This level has a direct link to the immune system of the body, and it is the heart of our physical health manifestations. The archangel associated with this level is Raphael, who is known as the angel of brightness, beauty, and *healing*. This level can be crucial to the turnaround of many systemic problems.

Geburah

Basic Color: Red.

Astrological Influence: Mars.

Healing Archangel: Kamael (Kah-Mah-Ehl).

Body Functions Influenced: The activities and the production of red corpuscles, the muscles of the body (voluntary and involuntary), the male sex organs, the reproductive system, excretory organs, prostrate gland, colon.

Geburah is a level of the subconscious mind that should be activated in times of feverish conditions and inflammatory disease. In times of surgery and accidents, this level can stimulate greater strength and recuperative powers.

This level has ties to the blood within the body, especially the production of red corpuscles. In cases of anemia, stimulating this level can be beneficial. Infections in the bloodstream can be affected through this level of the subconscious, along with deep-seated diseases.

Chesed

Basic Color: Blue.

Astrological Influence: Jupiter.

Healing Archangel: Tzadkiel (Zahd-Ki-Ehl).

Body Functions Influenced: Blood (venous activity), liver, cell nutrition, hips and thighs, buttocks, cerebral hemispheres, intestines.

Chesed is that level of the subconscious mind that mediates cell nutrition. It is a level connected to the body's ability to detoxify the blood system—one of the functions of the liver, which is ruled by Jupiter.

Problems with weight, too much or too little, can be influenced by stimulating and working with this level. This includes obesity as well as anorexia. With more and more food stuffs having less vitamin and mineral content, this is a level we need to stimulate regularly. It enables us to extract as much nutrition as possible from what we eat.

Binah

Basic Color: Black.

Astrological Influence: Saturn.

Healing Archangel: Tzaphkiel (Zahf-Ki-Ehl).

Body Functions Influenced: Skin, bones, teeth, joints, hearing, spleen, proper functioning of tendons and cartilage, gallbladder.

Binah is a powerful center to stimulate if you wish to decrease recovery time from illness. It is a dynamic center to stimulate at times of colds, chills, and rheumatism. It has an effect upon congestion in the body and the ossification of the bones. It can be stimulated to ease arthritis.

Binah is a level of the subconscious mind that can be stimulated to either ease the transition from life to death or to override fatal diseases, accidents, etc. Stimulating it can facilitate getting past a critical point in an illness.

Chokmah

Basic Color: Gray.

Astrological Influence: Neptune.

Healing Archangel: Ratziel (Rah-Tzi-Ehl).

Body Functions Influenced: Pineal gland, nervous system, cones and rods of the eyes, mental illness, lymph glands, the feet, nerve synapses in the brain.

This is a level of the subconscious that strongly affects the entire lymphatic system of the body. This includes all of the glands, their functions, and their connections to the chakras. It can be stimulated to ease allergic conditions and to identify their source. This level can also help us in handling contagious diseases, and it can assist us with physical problems associated with addictive behaviors (drugs, alcohol, etc.). It can be activated to ease colds and mucus conditions.

This subconscious level can also assist all psychological therapies. It is directly linked to our mental health, as it influences physical conditions. It can be awakened to reveal the metaphysical causes of physical conditions. It can enable us to see more clearly.

Kether

Basic Color: White.

Astrological Influence: Uranus.

Healing Archangel: Metatron (Meh-Tuh-Tron).

Body Functions Influenced: Regenerative forces of the reproductive system, body oxygenation, ankles, most syndromes, electrical impulses in the cells, the nervous system, spinal cord, some aspects of vision.

This can be a very important level of the subconscious when working with our health. Activating this level can bring clarification of symptoms and problems that previously could not be identified. Many syndromes are difficult to define, but this is a level that can facilitate drawing out the right information.

This level of the subconscious can positively influence many nervous disorders and ease conditions stemming from "incurable" problems and complaints. When stimulated properly, this level can also ease glaucoma and cataracts.

Tree of Life Healing Techniques

There are many techniques for using the Tree of Life in healing work—even in color healing. As we will see in the next chapter, there are four sets of color for each level of the Tree of Life. Each of these colors activates a level of the subconscious mind in its own specific manner.

In the previous pages, we gave only one basic healing color for each Qabalistic level. This basic color stimulates the subconscious mind in a way that opens it more effectively to the imaginative faculty, to the creative powers of the mind. It is a color that stimulates the creative energies at that level of the subconscious.

The single colors also help us to connect specifically to the healing ministrations of the archangel most associated with the subconscious level we are healing. We can thus experience the healing energies more tangibly. This does not mean other colors discussed in the next chapter are ineffective. Rather, it means that for each level, the color correspondence already cited is the color that is most definable in its healing effects when used with Tree of Life meditations, creative imagination, and healing archangels. Here is a good procedure to begin familiarizing yourself with the Tree of Life:

1. Begin by deciding which level of the Tree of Life you need to activate to assist you with your specific health problem.

2. Decide how you wish to incorporate the color: through candles, projected lights, color breath-

Conscious Mind

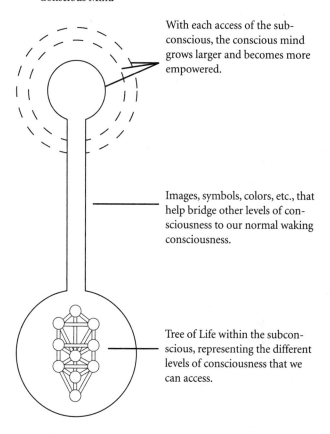

With each access of the sub-conscious, the conscious mind grows larger and becomes more empowered.

Images, symbols, colors, etc., that help bridge other levels of consciousness to our normal waking consciousness.

Tree of Life within the subconscious, representing the different levels of consciousness that we can access.

Subconscious Mind

Tapping Our Hidden Levels

In the Qabala color meditation techniques, we use colors to stimulate specific levels of the subconscious mind. This enables us to more effectively direct body processes and alter health factors that are controlled by that level of the mind.

ing, color swatches, or just visualization. You may use these in any combination, as you see fit. Since this is a healing meditation, you may wish to light candles (of the appropriate color) and fill the meditation area with that color vibration.

3. Close your eyes and perform a progressive relaxation. Begin slow, rhythmic breathing. See and feel yourself breathing the purest air possible. This strengthens and balances you.

4. Now, as you continue breathing slowly and regularly, visualize the air you inhale as changing to the color and vibrancy of the appropriate level in the Tree of life. See your body and your aura filling with this color. As you do this, visualize, imagine, and create within your own mind the scene that follows. The color you use in this meditation is one that activates the creative powers of the mind. This enhances the imaginative faculty and facilitates the opening of the corresponding level of subconsciousness.

You begin to see in your mind's eye a scene. You are standing in a meadow. The day is cloudy; gray tints the whole scene. There are flowers in the meadow, but they are either drooping or not in bloom. They mimic how you feel on some level.

In the middle of this meadow is a large tree. Its roots extend deep into the heart of the earth itself, and its upper branches are lost in the gray skies above. As large as it is, even the tree seems to droop.

You slowly walk toward it, and you see a small opening at its base. From this opening comes a soft light, the color you visualized at the beginning of this meditation. It is the color of the Tree of Life level you need to activate to help strengthen your own health.

You briefly pause and then step inside the tree. The inside is warm and comfortable. It shines with the soft color of the level you were seeking. It is comforting, and you deeply breathe in the color. It relaxes and soothes.

In the center is an altar upon which burns an eternal flame, a reminder to see this place as a temple within your own mind. The flame is small and soft, flickering occasionally. You notice, as you relax and absorb the color of this temple, the flame stabilizes and grows stronger. The altar is bordered by two pillars, reminders to maintain balance in your life.

In front of the altar is a soft light, hovering as if waiting to be called forth. You remember the healing archangel to whom you have access through this level of your mind. Softly, in a whisper, you speak the archangelic name, syllable by syllable. The light grows stronger.

You speak the name again—this time with more confidence. The light shifts and dances and begins to take form. You are beginning to see a glowing outline of a great figure.

Yet a third time, you speak the name—toning it strongly. The light shimmers, brightens, and then crystallizes: before you now stands a magnificent being of beauty and light. The energy radiating from this great being is like wings enveloping the entire inner temple. It touches you and lifts your heart.

The flame upon the altar grows stronger, brightening and illuminating the temple. The colors of the temple crystallize with diamondlike brilliance.

You hear your name softly spoken in your mind. You raise your eyes to this wondrous archangel. The eyes hold you; you are transfixed. Those eyes are older than time, and they are filled with such strength and unconditional love!

As the eyes stare into your own eyes, images begin to fill your mind. Strange and unfamiliar at first, you soon begin to recognize your own body—from the inside! You are being shown where the problem lies and how it affects other organs and systems of the body.

You begin to hear voices—your own and those of others. You see whole scenarios being acted out and see what the repercussions are for your own body. You begin to see the emotions and mental attitudes (of yourself and others) that have contributed to your condition.

As the images fade, this archangel steps forward. The wings of energy fan the air, filling it with the brilliant colors. You are embraced and a kiss is placed upon your head. Shivers of delight run throughout your body and soul. You see and feel yourself filling with the colors of the temple. You see and feel yourself restored to perfect balance. You are filled with exquisite joy and energy.

As the great being steps back, you see the temple fill with even greater intensities of the color, a reminder to you of the infinite health and energy available to you. Gently, you reach out with your heart and mind, daring to touch and thank this magnificent one. For a brief moment, you feel one with this being, and you know your health will only continue to improve, second by second, day by day, from this time forth.

The archangel steps back behind the altar and begins to recede from view. With the archangel gone, the altar is again completely visible. The light upon it now shines strong and brilliant and steady. This lamp reflects your own health. As you use these inner temples to balance and strengthen yourself, the inner lamps will grow brighter and shine more strongly within you.

You deeply breathe the energy of this inner temple, feeling yourself strong and rejuvenated. You are healthy and balanced, and it is this renewed health that you carry out of the Tree of Life into the physical world.

As you step outside the Tree, you are surprised. The gray skies are gone. Sunlight fills the meadow, warming and soothing all within it. The meadow flowers are in full bloom and color. The entire meadow looks as if it has been washed with every color of the rainbow.

You turn to look back at the tree. No longer does it droop. It is strong, tall, and vibrant. It is filled with new buds and bright green leaves.

You breathe in the crisp air. The image of the meadow fills your heart and your mind. You know that this is the reflection of your restored state of health. It is this which you have awakened and created and which you now bring back with you to your present surroundings. You have learned to stimulate the subconscious to create the gift of health and vibrancy.

Ten ▷ Colors of the Four Worlds

As we have discussed, the human essence is composed of more than just physical energies and processes. We operate on more than just a physical level. Our emotional, mental, and spiritual states are intimately entwined with our physical being.

The human mind is linked to all of our dimensions. We must remember, though, that our mind is not located in the brain. Yes, there is an intimate connection between the mind and the brain, but the mind is the seat of our consciousness.

The different levels of the subconscious mind not only influence physical body functions, but they give us access to the consciousness of other planes and dimensions as well. They integrate our emotional, mental, and spiritual states into physical expression. This is why, in holistic healing, the individual always looks for the metaphysical cause behind a physical problem.

Learning to work with the mind and affect it from all levels—physical, emotional, mental, and spiritual—is the key to establishing balanced health. This can be accomplished through color healing techniques—especially when utilizing a Qabalistic system of colors.

In the previous chapter we dealt with only one basic color for activating the different levels of the subconscious mind depicted in the Tree of Life. That color stimulated the imaginative faculty of the subconscious in a manner that opened us to the healing ministrations of the archangels operating around us.

There are other colors associated with each of the ten levels in the Tree of Life. Traditionally, the Tree of Life is divided into four worlds. These four worlds correspond to the physical, the emotional (astral), the mental, and the spiritual. The Four Worlds diagram (on the next page) shows one way we can look at this process. In this diagram, different levels of the subconscious give us access to different planes and energies.

A truer depiction of how this operates can be found in The Tree of Life in All Four Worlds diagram (page 145). In this depiction, each of the ten levels of the subconscious mind can be seen as operating on four levels. Each has a level within it that influences physical, emotional, mental, and spiritual aspects, respectively. For example, the level of the subconscious mind called Malkuth can be seen to have four dimensions within it—each affecting and being affected by specific physical, emotional, mental, and spiritual conditions. The same is true for each of the other nine levels.

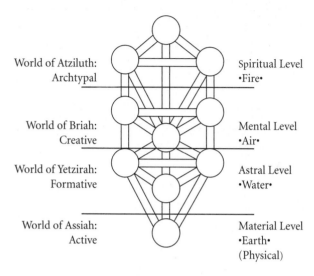

World of Atziluth: Spiritual Level
      Archtypal   •Fire•

World of Briah: Mental Level
       Creative   •Air•

World of Yetzirah: Astral Level
      Formative   •Water•

World of Assiah: Material Level
        Active   •Earth•
                             (Physical)

The Four Worlds

There are also four specific colors associated with each level. We can use all four colors to affect physical conditions, as well as their metaphysical causes. When we do, we are no longer working with a bandage-type healing, but are operating more holistically.

We can use these colors to help ease emotional, mental, and even spiritual imbalances. Just as there are physical functions of the body that are mediated by each level of the subconscious mind in the Tree of Life, so too are various emotional, mental, and spiritual states.

In the previous chapter we discussed the basic body functions mediated by each of the levels. There are certain nonphysical states that are more likely to create an imbalance in that level of the subconscious mind, helping to manifest specific physical imbalances. In this chapter, we will explore those emotional, mental, and spiritual states that can aggravate or interfere with the proper mediation of body functions at each level of the subconscious mind. We will then learn to use the complete color scheme to correct the emotional or mental imbalances, before they manifest as physical problems.

There is a chart on the following page giving the four dimensions within each level of the subconscious mind (as depicted in the Tree of Life). With a little practice and experimentation, you will find ways to use them in order to ease physical problems and the related metaphysical causes.

Throughout the rest of this chapter we will describe the various nonphysical states that affect the ten levels of the subconscious mind and their corresponding physical states. We will also explore several ways of using the color scheme to effect healing on all levels.

For example, from the previous chapter we know that the level of the subconscious we call Yesod affects menstruation. If you are having difficulty with menstrual cramps or PMS, more so than usual, you may wish to look at the nonphysical states that may create problems or aggravate physical conditions mediated by Yesod. Have you been dealing with sexual issues recently? Have you expressed or been exposed to arrogance? Has vanity been an issue recently?

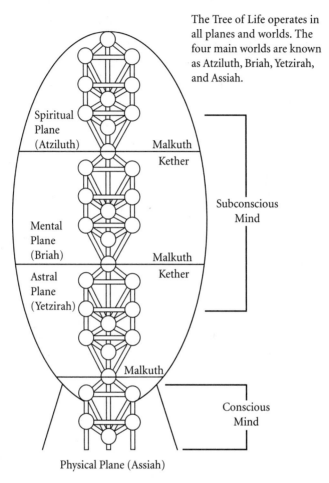

The Tree of Life operates in all planes and worlds. The four main worlds are known as Atziluth, Briah, Yetzirah, and Assiah.

Spiritual Plane (Atziluth)

Malkuth

Kether

Subconscious Mind

Mental Plane (Briah)

Malkuth

Kether

Astral Plane (Yetzirah)

Malkuth

Conscious Mind

Physical Plane (Assiah)

The Tree of Life in All Four Worlds

Even if you can't identify a nonphysical state that may have contributed to a particular condition, it is a good idea to use the complete color scheme. This ensures balance on all levels. (Sometimes it is easy to overlook possibilities and objectively evaluate what we have been feeling.)

The inverse is also true. If you can identify which emotions and mental attitudes (the nonphysical states) you have experienced or have been exposed to, it is easier to identify where a physical problem is more likely to manifest. We can then use the colors on a regular basis to prevent the determined level from becoming so out of balance that a physical problem manifests.

Malkuth

Malkuth is adversely affected by specific nonphysical states. These include laziness, greed, and avarice. Recklessness, aggression, and lack of discernment can cause or reflect problems in this level of the subconscious as well. And they can eventually lead to physical problems in areas discussed in the previous chapter. A lack of physical activity and never acting upon one's planning can also create imbalances in this level of the mind.

Yesod

The physical body functions mediated by Yesod can also be adversely affected by nonphysical states. These include idleness, emotional stress or imbalance, problems with

The Color Scheme of the Four Worlds

Level	Spiritual	Mental	Astral	Physical
Kether	Brilliance	White Brilliance	White Brilliance	White with Gold
Chokmah	Soft Blue	Gray	Mother of Pearl	White with Red, Blue, Yellow
Binah	Crimson	Black	Dark Brown	Gray with Pink
Chesed	Deep Violet	Blue	Deep Purple	Azure with Yellow
Geburah	Orange	Scarlet	Bright Scarlet	Red with Black
Tiphareth	Pink Rose	Yellow	Salmon	Amber
Netzach	Amber	Emerald	Yellow-Green	Olive with Gold
Hod	Violet Purple	Orange	Red Russet	Yellow-Brown
Yesod	Indigo	Violet	Dark Purple	Citrine with Azure
Malkuth	Yellow	Black, Olive, Russet, Citrine	Black, Olive, Russet, Citrine with Gold flecks	Black-rayed Yellow

sexuality, and vanity. A lack of confidence and independence can reflect a need for work on this level of the mind with the whole color scheme.

Hod

The physical functions of the body mediated by Hod can be adversely affected by deceit and dishonesty. Impatience, criticalness, and aloofness can also manifest with physical problems in those body functions controlled by this level of the subconscious mind. Difficulty with speech and communication, a lack of precision, and impractical behaviors can also cause or reflect a need for some color balancing.

Netzach

Lust and impurity, along with dramatic emotionalism, can create imbalances in this level of the mind, affecting the previously specified physical functions. Being exposed to possessiveness, introversion, jealousy, and defeatism can reflect a need for color balancing through this level's fourfold scheme. Expressing any of those qualities can also indicate the need for color balancing at this level. Antisocial behavior and lack of emotional control can also reflect or cause imbalances.

Tiphareth

Being exposed to or experiencing certain nonphysical states can adversely affect how this level mediates physical activities of the body. Anger is very detrimental, as is insecurity and false pride. A lack of compassion and mistrust can also reflect a need for working with the entire color scheme of this level. A pessimistic view on most things will often indicate a need for healing and balancing this level of the subconscious mind.

Geburah

This is a level that is often more easily identifiable as needing healing work. Hostility and fear often reflect imbalances and can cause physical problems in those areas of body activity mediated by Geburah. Hyperactivity, bullying, timidity, and a surrendering attitude can also create problems. A lack of confidence and a lack of critical judgment can create imbalances as well, thus requiring a full color scheme healing.

Chesed

Those body functions mediated and controlled by Chesed can also be adversely affected by nonphysical states. This includes expressions of hypocrisy, stinginess, self-righteousness, and the state of being overly conservative. An individual who is slow to respond or melancholy may eventually manifest imbalances in those physical areas mediated by this level. In such cases, the use of the fourfold color scheme will help restore balance.

Binah

This level of the subconscious can also be affected by nonphysical states, which in turn will affect those body functions mediated by it. Fear can be a major concern at this level, especially fear of the dark and of the future. An individual who is introverted may need to work with the whole color scheme, as will anyone who is always sacrificing him- or herself. If there is a lack of confidentiality, a lack of nurturing, or a failure to understand and employ patience, problems can occur that can best be corrected by using the entire color scheme.

Chokmah

As with the others, certain nonphysical states can interfere with the proper functioning of this level of the subconscious mind. This in turn will affect those body functions mediated by it. Being overly superstitious or misguidedly futuristic can lead you into some problems down the road in those areas affected by this level. Constant tardiness, lateness, and inefficiency can reflect some imbalances. Being forgetful and shortsighted can reflect a need to use the fourfold color scheme to eliminate these problems as well as any physical repercussions.

Kether

A negative self-image, a lack of imagination, and an inability to initiate new things can create problems in this level of the subconscious mind. These then can show up as physical problems in those areas mediated by this level. Always seeking sympathy, easily feeling shame, feeling misunderstood, and a lack of tenderness can reflect imbalance in this level. Self-denial and becoming lost in the illusions of the imaginative world can also reflect a need to use the fourfold scheme of colors to correct and prevent physical manifestations from these imbalances.

Healing Techniques with the Fourfold Color Scheme

Working with all four colors for each level is a little more complicated than working with a single color. First, it is difficult to make colored slides for some of the combinations, and it is also difficult to find candles of the appropriate colors and combinations. This should not prevent you from attempting to work with the entire color scheme for each level, as it has a powerful healing effect.

In all four of the methods discussed below, it is most effective to begin by working with the color(s) associated with the physical. Then move to the astral, the mental, and end with the spiritual. (Refer to the chart on page 147.)

Examine the physical symptoms you are experiencing; then, using the information given in this chapter and the last, determine which level(s) of the Tree of Life you need to stimulate with color. Once this is decided, simply choose one of the following techniques:

Breathing the Four Dimensions

One of the best ways to work on yourself is through the technique of color breathing. Once you decide which level of the subconscious you need to stimulate, use the chart given earlier to determine the four colors that will effect healing on all dimensions.

Spend three to five minutes breathing each color in, visualizing the conditions stabilizing and being healed. Start with the physical dimension and move to the astral; move to the mental and end with the spiritual.

Simple Color Projection

We learned earlier that we can project color through our hands at whatever frequency we are mentally focused upon. This technique is especially effective when working on someone else.

Have the person sit with eyes closed, relaxing with his or her back to you. Place your hands two to three inches above the crown of this person's head. If you wish, you may find it more comfortable to rest your hands directly on the head.

Relax yourself and begin rhythmic breathing. As you breathe in, feel the energy drawing into your body through the top of your own head. See and feel the energy in the color associated with the physical level. Feel it moving toward your hands to be projected outward.

Continue your rhythmic breathing. As you exhale, see and feel this colored energy pouring out your hands and down through the crown of the individual's head, filling the body. See it balancing, soothing, and healing the specific condition, while strengthening that level of the person's subconscious mind.

Continue for three to five minutes, or until you feel comfortable with it.

Now, pull your hands away and shake them briefly to clear the energy field. As you resume your rhythmic breathing, see and feel yourself filling with the colored energy of the astral level. See and feel yourself pouring forth this energy to fill the being and essence of the other individual.

Repeat this procedure for the color(s) of the mental and spiritual aspects as well. You have touched all four dimensions within that particular level of the subconscious mind. Your work has been holistic, treating physical and metaphysical imbalances.

Candle Healing on All Dimensions

We can adapt the techniques of candle healing to the Qabala, but it takes effort to find the variety of colored candles needed. In fact, you may not even find multi-color candles, as is often necessary for the physical dimension of a level.

It can be just as effective to use the predominant color. A little creativity and flexibility goes a long way and does not diminish the healing effects. For example, on the physical dimension of the subconscious level of Malkuth, the color is a black-rayed yellow. Using just a yellow candle (since it is the predominant color) is still effective.

After gathering the candles, sit or lie down on the floor. Put the candle with the color for the physical dimension in front of you, and the candle for the spiritual dimension behind you. On one side of you place the astral candle; on the other side, the mental candle.

Begin by lighting just the physical candle. See and feel its energy illuminating the area and being absorbed by the body, restoring balance. Next, light the astral. See and feel the emotional causes and effects of the illness being balanced. Then light the mental candle and imagine the mental attitudes that facilitated the problem being resolved and healed. Finally, light the spiritual dimension candle for the level you are working on. See it strengthening the effects of the others, and stabilizing your entire energy system.

Focus on each candle for three to five minutes. This is a powerful healing technique, and rarely takes more than three such treatments for a noticeable effect to be experienced. Wait at least twelve hours before repeating.

Awakening the Tree of Life

This technique takes a little longer to actually perform. You can do it for yourself through visualization and rhythmic breathing. It can also be performed on another person. It should not be attempted until extended periods of rhythmic breathing have been practiced, as it may cause hyperventilation.

Have the individual lie down, face up. Begin your own rhythmic breathing to build energy. Place your hands at the crown of the other person's head. This is Kether, the top of the Tree of Life. See and feel the energy pouring through your hands into this area of the body. Begin with the color for the physical dimension, and then move to the astral, mental, and spiritual.

When you have done all the colors for Kether, move your hands down to the left side of the face, and begin sending the colors for Chokmah. Do the same for Binah and all of the others, down to the feet (Malkuth). See the diagram, Awakening the Tree of Life (on the next page).

This path draws energy all through the body, while activating all levels of the subconscious mind. It takes a little longer to perform, but it is very catalytic in effecting healing changes.

A beneficial variation of this is to make four passes from top to bottom along the so-called Path of the Flaming Sword. Begin by using all of the physical dimension colors for each level; then, start back at the top and go through all of the astral colors, followed by the mental and the spiritual colors. Do the same for each level.

You will see and feel a noticeable difference when working on someone in this manner. Your energy will build. While you are helping to build and balance the other person's energies, you are also building and strengthening the entire Tree of Life within your energy field. It remains strong and vibrant within the aura, and it helps make you less susceptible to imbalance. It is a wonderful healing tonic when used on a regular basis.

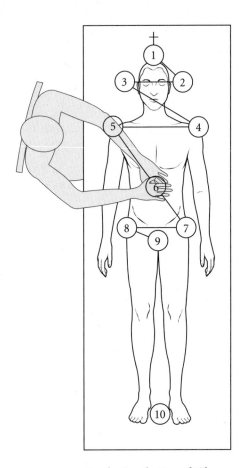

Awakening the Tree of Life

By sending energy along the ancient Path of the Flaming Sword,* you acti-vate a powerfully creative force. You draw it down through the body, affect-ing all systems and all levels of energy.

---

* For more information on the Path of the Flaming Sword, consult the author's earlier works on the Qabala: *Simplified Qabala Magic* and *Imagick*.

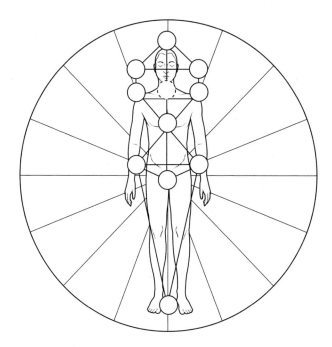

The Tree of Life Within the Aura

When the Tree of Life is built into the aura through healing, the aura begins to shine with new color, clarity, and vibrancy.

Eleven

Color Healing Mandalas

Color has been used in many ways throughout the history of humanity to express, to heal, and to illumine. It was an essential aspect of sacred art. Sacred art used color to create designs that would expand consciousness. It was believed that colors stimulated the outer eyes in a manner that awakened the inner eyes.

The mandala is the most commonly known form of sacred art. It is a tool for focusing the mind. A mandala holds the essence of a specific thought or concept. Through its design and color scheme, it draws the consciousness more fully into that concept. It creates unity. Because disease or illness reflects a breakdown in the holistic unity of the body, the mandala can be a powerful tool for color healing.

In Eastern philosophy, mandalas are commonly known as *yantras*. They are known as medicine shields in the Native American tradition. They can be a mélange of geometric patterns, colors, and designs created to elicit specific effects. For our purposes, we will use the term *mandala* to include all of its forms.

Mandalas stimulate the inner creative forces in a manner peculiar to their design. They can be constructed to arouse any inner force or desire. They are symbols for integration and transformation, a form of action and interaction within ourselves.

Mandalas serve to stimulate the primal inner sources imprinted within the deeper levels of the mind—including the inner source of our own healing. They are psychic transformers, helping us to connect with our missing parts.

Healing mandalas are designs with symbols and colors that are used to create shifts in our energy on physical and/or subtle levels. All colors, all symbols, and all geometric shapes alter our electromagnetic field. In chapter 8 we discussed how certain geometric shapes can be used in candle layouts to amplify and effect healing. In constructing and meditating with mandalas, we are doing the same thing.

All healing mandalas work best when made personally. The more you know about what their various symbols represent, the more receptive you will be to their influence. Constructing and coloring a mandala is itself an act of healing. It is an act of taking charge, of participating in the responsibility for your own health. The essence of art therapy has ties to this ancient concept of sacred art.

There are many methods of creating healing mandalas. This book is not the forum for exploring all of the

intricacies. Instead, we will focus on some simple mandala designs that you can use to begin to have an impact
upon your own health. Do not limit yourself strictly to
the symbols and designs given in the rest of this chapter.
They are merely guidelines to offer you a starting point
for creating your own healing art.

Creating a Color Wheel

A color wheel is a tool that helps you to be more sensitive
to colors and their healing aspects. Because you are working with the full spectrum of colors, you are able to balance and heal yourself just by constructing it. Creating a
color wheel for yourself is simple:

1. Draw a circle about six to seven inches in diame-
   ter.

2. Using a protractor, mark off a point every thirty
   degrees, and then divide the circle into twelve
   equal parts. (You do not have to limit yourself
   to twelve. You can make it four or seven or however many you wish.)

3. Then, using colored pencils, paints, or markers,
   color in each section. Start with red and then
   move through the shades to violet (see the Basic
   Color Wheel illustration, page 163). You used to
   enjoy coloring as a child; do so again.

4. Notice how you feel as you color each section.
   Do you feel more drawn to some colors and not
   others? How does each color look when you

place another color next to it? Do some of the colors make you feel better than others? Do you enjoy coloring with some shades more than others? All of these questions can provide clues to which colors are beneficial to your current health state.

5. Now create another color wheel; but change the arc that serves as each section's outer perimeter. It can be a bulbous wheel or a diamond-shaped wheel. How does the shape change the way you feel about the colors as you fill in the wheel? Try experimenting with different colors this time around, too. Note the effects each color has on you.

Creating Healing Mandalas

Mandalas that are most effective for healing are personal to the user. This means you choose the colors according to the effects you wish to stimulate. You also choose the design and symbols according to your purpose. Determine in advance what purpose the mandala is to serve.

You can make a new mandala each time a problem surfaces. Or, if you desire, you can make a more universal one to use in healing meditations—one that you use on a regular basis to sustain good health. Both have their benefits. When you make a new mandala each time, it keeps you involved in a creative and joyful act, which in itself is healing. Mandalas that are used over extended periods of time de-

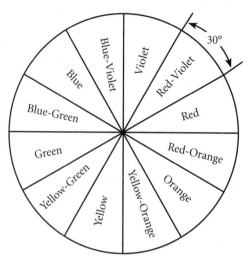

Basic Color Wheel

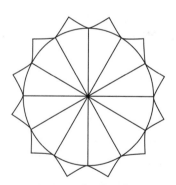

Augmented Color Wheel

Creating Color Wheels and Variations

velop a thoughtform of healing around them—their effects become stronger each time they are employed.

Whichever way you decide to go with this, make sure you keep in mind the mandala's purpose as you construct it. The more significance you attach to the colors, symbols, and designs, the more they will be able to work for you.

Mandalas can be made from almost any material. Simple poster board is inexpensive and easy to work with. Be sure to make it large enough so that you can see all aspects of it when it is across the room from you.

Healing mandalas are very effective when constructed within a circular shape. We can use other geometric forms inside of that circle, but the circle is a good symbol of wholeness and unity, which is what you are trying to achieve with the healing.

Review the effects of the geometric shapes as discussed in chapter 8 (page 110). Examine some of the other healing mandala forms and the effects they elicit, as given in the following pages. Choose the symbols and shapes that you need and that will activate the energies you desire through the mandala.

Then, experiment with various layouts within the circumference of your mandala circle. Make the layout as meaningful as possible. A dozen different people may use the same symbols and even the same colors, but the way they will be placed in the mandala will vary from individual to individual. This is as it should be.

For an example of a general healing mandala, refer to the A Healing Mandala illustration on the next page. It uses the symbols and shapes given in this book. It is strengthening and stabilizing to the entire metabolism of the body. It is also beneficial to the immune system, having a dynamic effect upon the heart chakra. Its effectiveness is enhanced when opposite colors are used. (Refer to the Opposite Colors chart, page 49).

The color in the mandala can also be made more personal to you through some simple correspondences. You can use the colors associated with major aspects of your

This simple healing mandala uses only three symbols: the circle, an elongated six-rayed star, and the bindhu. It stabilizes and activates the heart chakra. It draws the meditator into it—into a new state of balance.

A Healing Mandala

astrological chart. (The three most important aspects are your sun, moon, and rising signs. The colors for these three help to restore your basic energy pattern.)

Alphabet Color Correspondences

Letters	Colors	Letters	Colors
A	White	N	Blue-Green
B	Yellow	O	Black
C	Red-Orange	P	Scarlet
D	Emerald	Q	Violet
E	Blue	R	Orange
F	Light Red-Orange	S	Blue
		T	Green-Yellow
G	Deep Blue	U	Earth Tones
H	Bright Reds	V	Red Orange
I	Red-Violet	W	Green, Silver
J	Yellow-Green	X	Deep Indigo
K	Blue-Violet	Y	Light Golden Brown
L	Emerald	Z	Pastel Orange
M	Mother of Pearl		

Healing Mandala Symbols

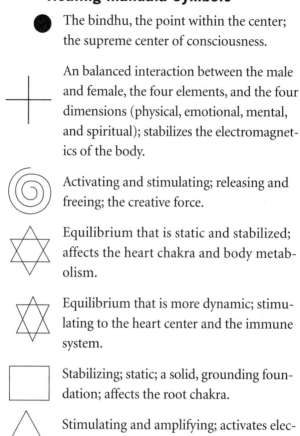

The bindhu, the point within the center; the supreme center of consciousness.

An balanced interaction between the male and female, the four elements, and the four dimensions (physical, emotional, mental, and spiritual); stabilizes the electromagnetics of the body.

Activating and stimulating; releasing and freeing; the creative force.

Equilibrium that is static and stabilized; affects the heart chakra and body metabolism.

Equilibrium that is more dynamic; stimulating to the heart center and the immune system.

Stabilizing; static; a solid, grounding foundation; affects the root chakra.

Stimulating and amplifying; activates electrical aspects; fiery and masculine.

Grounding; activates the magnetic aspects of the body; watery and feminine.

Egyptian Symbols of Healing

 Symbol of Isis: can be used for all female issues of health and to assist children.

 The eye of Horus: Beneficial for all physical healing; preventive medicine.

 The sistrum: a symbol for Bast and beneficial for identifying the mental causes of physical illness; beneficial to mental health.

 The caduceus, a symbol for Thoth: this is the symbol for amplifying any and all of the healing arts; in meditation it helps determine the karma of disease.

 The symbol for Sirius: activates strength and stamina; opens the unconscious to healing energy.

 Hieroglyphs: life, health, and prosperity, respectively.

 The Ankh: the symbol of the life force; gently strengthens the healing energies.

Other traditions have their own symbols that can be used in healing mandalas. This is but one example of a set of healing symbols. A little study of other traditions will reveal much about their healing symbols.

Your name is also a powerful energy signature. The various elements in your name (the vowels and consonants) have specific colors associated with them. These colors are symbolic of specific energies that you have chosen to work with on some other level. They are also very stabilizing to your overall energy system, physical and otherwise. Using the chart on page 166, you can incorporate your name's colors into your mandala, amplifying the effects of the mandala for you.

Healing Mandala Meditation

When you reach a point in constructing your mandala where you are unsure of what to add next, stop. You have probably created what is appropriate for you at this time.

When you have finished with it, set it across from you about four to five feet away. Just sit and gaze at it for about ten to fifteen minutes. Feel its energies. Visualize everything it will do for you. Review its meanings. Ask yourself questions as you gaze upon it. Does it need other colors? Do you find it peaceful and calming? Energizing?

Try to imagine the energy flowing off this mandala in healing waves to surround and embrace you. Close your eyes, visualizing it within your mind. As you sit across from it with your eyes closed, what part of your body feels it most strongly?

As you sit across from it, relaxing, see it floating off of the board in waves of energy to overlay your body. See yourself in the middle of the mandala, absorbing it into your own body. Visualize this mandala shining with strength and vibrancy within you. Feel it encompassing your entire aura with healing energies. Know that each time you look upon it, or picture it in your mind, it will automatically begin to work for you.

As you work with the mandalas and all of the techniques outlined in this book, you will begin to see colors from an entirely different perspective. Each time you see any color, you will recognize that it truly is a luminescent energy. You will begin to see it as an outward reflection of the light within.

Twelve

Holistic Health

Anyone can heal. Anyone can learn to administer energies that accelerate and facilitate the healing process. This can be done physically, emotionally, mentally, and spiritually. The human essence is a wondrous thing. Its capacity to rejuvenate and regenerate itself is limited solely by our awareness. The amount of healing energy available to each of us is limited solely by our capacity to give love and respect every day to ourselves and others.

Many methods of healing and doctoring exist. Everyone that you speak to has a different opinion as to which is best. The truth is that the best one is the one that works for you. Each of us has a unique energy system, and to generalize and lump all symptoms and all problems (and their respective cures) into one category does a great disservice to us as individuals and to humanity as a whole.

Part of our responsibility as an individual human being is to find that method or combination of methods that works best for us as individuals. This involves time and study, something many are still not willing to do in our present society. There is a tendency to relegate the responsibility for our bodies and the knowledge of them to outside individuals. But healing begins with learning about our own physical bodies, their organs and systemic functions.

Above the portals of the ancient mystery temples— the centers of higher learning, healing, and spirituality—were but two words: "Know Thyself." A simple enough axiom, it is one that creates tremendous difficulty for many. People are unwilling to take the time to know themselves; thus they give that responsibility over to others. They hire individuals to "know" for them.

All healing comes from within. And the more you know about your body, the more you can participate in the healing process. The body—physical and otherwise— has a tremendous capacity for restoring itself to health. Yes, because of genetics and such influences as karma, there can be a greater predisposition or preconditioning to various problems. Traditional medicine and doctoring may serve as a catalyst to correct the problem, but it often does not correct the cause of the problem. Modern medicine is still unsure how various diseases manifest. Why do they affect some people and not others? What makes some individuals prone to illness and other problems? Words such as "virus," "bacteria," "weakened constitution," etc., are not really explanations. Viruses and bacteria surround us all the time, so why are we sick sometimes and not others?

This book is not a manual to replace orthodox medicine. The methods in here are not prescriptive. They are simply descriptions of energy applications that have been tried and found to have elicited results when previously used by others. These healing methods have been employed in combination with orthodox medical treatments, and on their own. I have used them in my own life for a variety of conditions—including my asthma.

All treatments, orthodox and otherwise, have function and viability. There are times when the orthodox medical approach (including surgery) is very necessary in the restoration of balance and health, but to make it exclusive as a treatment is to deny that you have any control or responsibility in your own health maintenance.

If nothing else, this manual should provide an opportunity to experience the innate subtleties of the human essence and to experience the healing ability that resides within each of us without exception. We each can assist with the healing of our bodies and our lives by expanding our perceptions, and increasing our knowledge and our personal responsibility.

Working with alternative and holistic traditions serves many functions. It opens our awareness of how we operate on more than just a physical level. It demonstrates tangibly and visibly that we can effect changes by using proper techniques. It shows us what we need to learn about ourselves, what we need to change about ourselves, and what we can control in ourselves.

Once experienced, our lives can never be the same. Everything in the world takes on greater significance. Every thought, word, and deed takes on a new importance as the interplay between your words and the physical body is understood and experienced. You begin to know that you can control much of what you experience in the line of dis-ease and ill health. You always have options. You become more aware of life and energy operating on all planes and dimensions within you and around you. You become aware that all is truly possible.

Part of what we must learn is that there is a divine spark within us. We are here in the physical world to learn that life is supposed to go right; we are here to learn how to make it right. People receive answers to their prayers or experience a healing, and they exclaim, "The most amazing thing happened!" The truth is, prayers are supposed to be answered. Miracles are supposed to happen. Healings are supposed to occur! The *amazing* thing would be if they did not occur.

When we were children, we had no limits. Everything was possible. We all need to see the world sparkle again, as if for the first time. There is still adventure, health, joy, and magic yet to be born within our lives. It is my hope that through the techniques of this book you experience a rebirth of the light and color within your own life, and that in turn you become a light unto others.

Bibliography

Buckland, Raymond. *Practical Candleburning Rituals.* St. Paul, MN: Llewellyn Publications, 1982.

———*Practical Color Magic.* St. Paul, MN: Llewellyn Publications, 1984.

Cosimano, Charles. *Psionics 101.* St. Paul, MN: Llewellyn Publications, 1987.

Crookall, Robert. *Psychic Breathing.* Hollywood, CA: Newcastle Publishing, 1985.

Judith, Anodea. *Wheels of Life.* St. Paul, MN: Llewellyn Publications, 1988.

Krieger, Dolores. *The Therapeutic Touch.* Englewood Cliffs, NJ: Prentice-Hall, 1976.

MacIvor, Virginia and Sandra LaForest. *Vibrations.* York Beach, ME: Samuel Weiser, 1979.

Nielsen, Greg and Joseph Polanski. *Pendulum Power.* New York: Warner Destiny Books, 1977.

Ouseley, S. G. J. *Colour Meditations.* Essex, England: L. N. Fowler and Co., Ltd., 1944.

Ramacharaka, Yogi. *Science of Breath.* Chicago: Yogi Publishing Society, 1905.

Schwarz, Jack. *Human Energy Systems.* New York: E. P. Dutton, 1980.

Vinci, Leo. *Candle Magic.* Northamptonshire: Aquarian Press, 1983.

Wilson, Annie and Lilla Bek. *What Colour Are You?* Northamptonshire: Turnstone Press, 1982.

Zi, Nancy. *The Art of Breathing.* New York: Bantam Books, 1986.

GET MORE AT LLEWELLYN.COM

Visit us online to browse hundreds of our books and decks, plus sign up to receive our e-newsletters and exclusive online offers.

- **Free tarot readings • Spell-a-Day • Moon phases**
- **Recipes, spells, and tips • Blogs • Encyclopedia**
- **Author interviews, articles, and upcoming events**

GET SOCIAL WITH LLEWELLYN

Find us on

Facebook
www.Facebook.com/LlewellynBooks

Follow us on
twitter
www.Twitter.com/Llewellynbooks

GET BOOKS AT LLEWELLYN

LLEWELLYN ORDERING INFORMATION

Order online: Visit our website at www.llewellyn.com to select your books and place an order on our secure server.

Order by phone:
- Call toll free within the U.S. at 1-877-NEW-WRLD (1-877-639-9753)
- Call toll free within Canada at 1-866-NEW-WRLD (1-866-639-9753)
- We accept VISA, MasterCard, and American Express

Order by mail:
Send the full price of your order (MN residents add 6.875% sales tax) in U.S. funds, plus postage and handling to: Llewellyn Worldwide, 2143 Wooddale Drive Woodbury, MN 55125-2989

POSTAGE AND HANDLING

STANDARD (U.S. & Canada):
(Please allow 12 business days)
$25.00 and under, add $4.00.
$25.01 and over, FREE SHIPPING.

INTERNATIONAL ORDERS (airmail only):
$16.00 for one book, plus $3.00 for each additional book.

Visit us online for more shipping options.
Prices subject to change.

FREE CATALOG!

To order, call
1-877-NEW-WRLD
ext. 8236
or visit our website

How To Meet & Work with Spirit Guides

TED ANDREWS

We often experience spirit contact in our lives but fail to recognize it for what it is. Now you can learn to access and attune to beings such as guardian angels, nature spirits and elementals, spirit totems, archangels, gods and goddesses—as well as family and friends after their physical death.

Contact with higher soul energies strengthens the will and enlightens the mind. Through a series of simple exercises, you can safely and gradually increase your awareness of spirits and your ability to identify them. You will learn to develop intentional and directed contact with any number of spirit beings. Discover meditations to open up your subconscious. Learn which acupressure points effectively stimulate your intuitive faculties. Find out how to form a group for spirit work, use crystal balls, perform automatic writing, attune your aura for spirit contact, use sigils to contact the great archangels, and much more! Read *How To Meet and Work with Spirit Guides* and take your first steps through the corridors of life beyond the physical.

0-7387-0812-7 $9.95

How To
Uncover Your Past Lives

Ted Andrews

How To Uncover Your Past Lives
TED ANDREWS

Knowledge of your past lives can be extremely rewarding. It can assist you in opening to new depths within your own psychological makeup. It can provide greater insight into present circumstances with loved ones, career, and health. It is also a lot of fun.

Now Ted Andrews shares with you nine different techniques that you can use to access your past lives. Between techniques, Andrews discusses issues such as karma—and how it is expressed in your present life; the source of past-life information, soul mates and twin souls, proving past lives, the mysteries of birth and death, animals and reincarnation, abortion and premature death, and the role of reincarnation in Christianity.

To explore your past lives, you need only use one or more of the techniques offered. Complete instructions are provided for a safe and easy regression. Learn to dowse to pinpoint the years and places of your lives with great accuracy, make your own self-hypnosis tape, attune to the incoming child during pregnancy, use the tarot and the Qabala in past-life meditations, keep a past-life journal, and more.

0-7387-0813-5 $8.95

How To See and Read the Aura

TED ANDREWS

Everyone has an aura—the three-dimensional, shape-and-color-changing energy field that surrounds all matter. And anyone can learn to see and experience the aura more effectively. There is nothing magical about the process. It simply involves a little understanding, time, practice, and perseverance.

Do some people make you feel drained? Do you find some rooms more comfortable and enjoyable to be in? Have you ever been able to sense the presence of other people before you actually heard or saw them? If so, you have experienced another person's aura. In this practical, easy-to-read manual, you receive a variety of exercises to practice alone and with partners to build your skills in aura reading and interpretation. Also, you will learn to balance your aura each day to keep it vibrant and strong so others cannot drain your vital force.

Learning to see the aura not only breaks down old barriers—it also increases sensitivity. As we develop the ability to see and feel the more subtle aspects of life, our intuition unfolds and increases, and the childlike joy and wonder of life returns.

0-7387-0815-1 $8.95

Animal-Speak

The Spiritual & Magical Powers of Creatures Great & Small

TED ANDREWS

The animal world has much to teach us. Some animals are experts at survival and adaptation, some never get cancer, and some embody strength and courage, while others exude playfulness. Animals remind us of the potential we can unfold, but before we can learn from them, we must first be able to speak with them.

In this book, myth and fact are combined in a manner that will teach you how to speak and understand the language of the animals in your life. *Animal-Speak* helps you meet and work with animals as totems and spirits—by learning the language of their behaviors within the physical world. It provides techniques for reading signs and omens in nature so you can open yourself to higher perceptions and even prophecy. It reveals the hidden, mythical, and realistic roles of forty-five animals, sixty birds, eight insects, and six reptiles.

Animals will become a part of you, revealing to you the majesty and divine in all life. They will restore your childlike wonder of the world and strengthen your belief in magic, dreams, and possibilities.

0-87542-028-1 $21.95